In my role in behavioural anal
am always seeking new ways
alive and be real in most peo
Vicky for some years now an

passion, her energy and boundless enthusiasm for the
subject to be quite irresistible. The simplicity of her
explanations are done in such a way to which everybody
can relate to. Reading this book will really make a
difference to how you see yourself and how you view
others.
Ron Knox
Sales Manager for Thomas International London

This book is a 'must have' for anyone who works with
people. Whether you are already trained in
communication skills or completely new to
understanding how behaviour is created, this book will
give you unique resources that will help you to make a
difference. As a Leadership Development Trainer I
highly recommend this book to my clients as it contains
gems of information which makes working with others
easier.
Fiona Campbell
True Business Leader Ltd

"A fantastic journey of self-discovery!"
Enter the world of your thoughts and feelings; find out
what they are really trying to tell you, and how you can
find the answers to the questions you have been
asking. This book is a must read for anyone who wants
to understand themselves. It tells you the facts and gives
you back your power, unlocking the secrets within our
everyday communication, enabling you to start making
positive changes to your life!"
Lisa Honey

This book is superb. It progresses the reader through the three parts, helping them grow. It explains how we think, how we feel and how to simplify our lives and be happy. As a teacher working with primary school children, this book has helped me better understand behavior in adults and children which I have found to be priceless. Everyone should read this book!
Sue Stephens
Teacher

iUnderstand Me takes the reader on a superb and enlightening journey in self-development and understanding. It embodies powerful messages in a very simple manner that will help a broad audience. It is an excellent guide to understanding yourself and how you perceive others. Vicky's unadulterated passion for sharing her expertise, knowledge and experience exudes throughout and everyone will benefit from this journey to self-awareness whether just starting their journey or those looking to advance along their path.
Nichola Crust
Head of Quality Assurance

iUnderstand Me

How to change your thoughts and beliefs to be happy

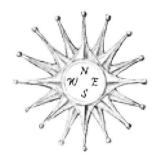

Vicky Ross

iUnderstand Me

How to change your thoughts and beliefs and be happy

Second Edition

Copyright © 2011

by Vicky Ross

ISBN 978-0-9570973-0-8

Published by KatGab Publishers

Kent, United Kingdom

www.katgabpublishers.com

Cover Design by Lisa Honey

Back page photo by Jane Collier

Printed in Great Britain by Orbital Print Ltd,

Sittingbourne, Kent

To Ian, Katerina and Gabrielle

You have helped me grow; you have put up with my endless curious mind and allowed me to discover the things that puzzled me. You have supported me when things changed and I was hitting a brick wall. You have stood by me without question. Most of all you have had the amazing patience for me to write it all out.

Thank you for giving me the platform to do what I love.

I love you all so much. This book is for you.

Contents

Acknowledgments

I am deeply grateful to everyone who has contributed to my life. I am sincerely thankful to my parents, my siblings and my friends. My journey of self development and understanding started some 30 years ago. From then I have been collecting theories and explanations to all that was happened in my life. My life offered me the lessons I needed to become the person I am today. One of the biggest turning points in my life was started by Colin Wingrove and his wife ... my Aussie mom. Thank you for helping me begin to understand myself. It was the start of my conscious awareness.

As Steve Jobs said: "*Of course it was impossible to connect the dots looking forward when I was in college. But it was very, very clear looking backwards ten years later. Again, you can't connect the dots looking forward; you can only connect them looking backwards. So you have to trust that the dots will somehow connect in your future.*"

On my path I have met many significant mentors and teachers. Some of them know me, some don't. Some of the knowledge that I have accrued as a result of my many years of study, can also be seen in the unit reader for the Introduction to Leadership and Management course that I have developed and co-authored for Bournemouth University.

Thank you to Dr Richard Bandler, John and Kathleen La Valle for having me as an assistant to all the NLP seminars in London. It gave me the opportunity to learn over and over again and fine tune my message.

To Paul McKenna for choosing me to join his team and putting me in an environment that helped me grow.

To Michael Neill for teaching me how to be a good teacher and a good speaker. Also for helping me understand that my message is important.

To Will Thomas who coached me, held me and supported me all the way through the writing of this book. Thank you for believing in me. You are awesome.

To Paul Hutchins for helping me to put out there a very clear message.

To Thomas Otten for playing the music to every word I wrote.

To Lisa who illustrated in such a perfect cover for my book, and for formatting and designing the book. You work and support has been very valuable to me.

To Sue for being such a great friend and for supporting me and helping me get this book to the finish line.

...and again to my friend, husband and lover Ian, for reading, editing alongside me and for always supporting and believing in me, my work and my purpose. You have offered me the platform I needed to grow.

Thank you to my wonderful girls for giving me all the time I needed to finish and for all the hours they watched me type rather than be with them. You are important to me, you mean the world to me and I love you very much.

What this book is all about?

This is book is everything about you! It is about your thinking, about your communication, your behaviour and your view of the world. It is about how you live your life.

This is about the hidden messages that give you clues to that mysterious part of your inner psyche, so that you can better understand yourself. It will teach you about your thoughts and beliefs and help you find inner peace. You will be able to understand your own inner dialogue and how this steers your behaviour, what motivates you and those around you and how to start making changes.

All our behaviour has a beginning and an end. We start to do something, we work through the process, and then we finish and move on to something else. Even doing nothing is something that we do. If we were not born with the behaviour, then it is fair to say we have learned it. When we are looking to change our lives, we need to change the way that we have always done things. We need to change the process that we are currently using. It is a bit like following a map. We start by going from one place to another and back again.

Back in history, people believed that there was an edge that if we passed we would fall off the earth. Brave people, pioneers of those times dared to tread past this perceived edge. To learn, to do something new, is like exploring new territory or taking a different road we become the pioneers of our own lives. We need to break new ground and find new paths to walk, so that we change the way we are doing things. Not all things need to change; some things give us the perfect results that we want. However, some things in life don't.

When we explore different pathways, we teach ourselves flexibility to do the same things in different ways. In other words in some ways we are getting the same results in a better way. We start to move towards the life that we want and leave behind the pain, struggle and suffering. To move forward with confidence one must have courage to embrace new things. They must be able to overcome fears and trust that there is enough knowledge inside of them to do the things that they want to do. So, is now a good time to start? Small steps or big leaps? Everyone is on their own journey and this book is there to guide and support you.

All that we feel, think and dream is inside of us. The only way that anyone can translate this into the world and share it with others is through language. Within this language there are patterns of speech and each pattern tells a story. When you learn to listen to those patterns and understand what they mean, they give you an insight to the speaker. That speaker may be you or it may be someone you are having a conversation with. This knowledge will enable you to better understand yourself and as a result you become a very skilled communicator.

How does this book fit into your life?

It does not matter what work you do, we all speak. Sometimes there is no need to do anything but just enjoy the conversation. However, there are times when clear and concise conversation is paramount to success at work or at home. This information gives you the edge to do what you have always done and more. You will be able to understand the motives and behaviours of yourself and those around you.

We live in an ever changing world and the key to success is to be able to communicate clearly to others as well as understand what they want. We naturally speak in an abstract and ambiguous way and for most of the time that works. However, that same system can cause miscommunication which results in most of the troubles that we have in our lives.

How to read this book:

This book is best read in the way that you need. There is no right or wrong way to read it. You can dip in and out as your knowledge expands or start from the beginning and work through all the sections. I know you will find the perfect way for you. It has the knowledge and information for all levels, whether you are a novice or an expert.

This book comes in three parts. Your own personal progress will determine where you should start.

However, I would recommend, irrespective of your background, to read through the whole book. It will strengthen any knowledge you already have. Each chapter will begin with what you will learn and what questions will be answered. From there in italics you will read the ramblings of the internal dialogue. That is followed by a summary of what you have learned till that point. Every chapter will end with an exercise for you to do.

Part One of the book, is for the novice. If you are new in the field of communication then this is your starting point.

You will learn:

- What communication is and what it isn't.
- What information about communication most of the western world is missing.
- What you can start to pay attention to that will make a difference to the skill of your communication.
- How to understand yourself better.

Part Two is for those of you that have attended an NLP course or any other communication course where you have been taught how to listen to language patterns. It will allow you to review what you already know or add to your existing knowledge.

You will learn:

- To begin to identify the different language patterns that we use to put content in.
- To listen to the speaker and how to interpret the deeper meaning of the language patterns used in speech.
- The relationship of the language patterns to the content.
- How to use skilful questioning skills, for the purpose of retrieving a deeper meaning from the information that is being presented.

Part Three is for those who have the academic knowledge but are not using it in their business or personal lives. There are a myriad of reasons why people do not put their academic knowledge into practice. The gap between knowledge of something and the doing of something is possibly the biggest frustration to anyone who has the information and yet defaults back to old patterns of behaviour.

What it shows is that on a deeper level the connection from knowledge to experience has not happened and that the learning cycle is not complete. When we know something, and I mean really know it, we use it. Not using the tools implies there are still gaps in the learning.

You will learn:

- How our emotions cloud our judgment.
- How we create behaviour and how that puts us back into default.
- How to disassociate and not distort the information given in order to stay resourceful.
- To bridge the gap between academia and practice and how to use all this information in the real world to become a successful communicator.

Part One

Michelle is on the start of her journey.

iUnderstand Me

Introduction

The easiest way to learn the art of interpretation and attain a deeper understanding of your own self is to observe it in others. When we observe it in others, we are able to remain emotionally unattached and unbiased. The success you get by practicing with others builds the confidence you need to feel so that you can use this more and more. In turn, you can start to listen to your inner voice and start unravelling all the mysteries you had about yourself, your behaviours, your beliefs and motives.

You often hear that the secret to good communication is to listen more effectively. However, as much as most people know that, they still seem to not be doing it.

> *So what is it that stops a person from succeeding in the art of listening?*

In order to listen effectively, you need to understand how the process of interpretation happens in our neurology, and how that process decodes words into chemical experiences in our body.

Yes, words in whatever language create a chemical response in the body and once you understand this sophisticated process, you start to understand how by listening more "effectively" you are able to know what 'behaviour drivers' a person has. To really become more effective in your listening and communication skills, you first have to understand what you are listening to.

Every word is a linguistic anchor. Every word has a meaning that we have attached to it and with that an emotion. So when we speak we induce meaning and emotions in others. Our internal dialogue induces the same process but this time it is in ourselves. The sad thing is, that the majority of the time, this is done unconsciously and, because we are not taught to think about our thinking: *to be the observer of our thoughts*, we start to think that our thoughts are real and as a result we begin to believe things about ourselves that are actually not true. They are just thoughts.

When we wake up from the daze of the unconscious living we start to realize that we are the owners and creators of our thoughts, we can take a step back and ask ourselves if these thoughts are useful to us right now. Without an acceptance and ownership of this concept and, without a conscious awareness of how we are feeling, we can't move to a place of freedom from the thoughts that imprison us from the life we want to live.

Guru: There is no happiness in the world I say...

Student: What, no happiness? What about all the people that are searching for happiness, peace, acceptance, love...?

Guru: Look outside the window, at the world. Do you see any of those things you mentioned?

Student: But where are they then? I don't understand! Where should I search?

Guru: Where it has always been, inside you. All that you want is within you. It is like your hidden treasure, once you find it you will have all that you asked for.

Chapter One - We Live in Two Worlds

In this chapter you will learn:

1. About the worlds that we create and how to understand them.

2. How to identify where our problems lie.

3. Where to start finding solutions.

4. What is going on with other people.

In this chapter you will be able to answer the following questions:

1. Where do I begin solving uncomfortable and awkward situations?

2. Why am I not getting answers from all the books and seminars?

3. What are my thoughts capable of?

4. How does my brain view experiences and thoughts?

I feel sad, and a little bored. I am restless. It is as if I need some drama in my life. I am after all the drama queen. If there is no drama I am sure to make some! I am not sure if it is my boredom that is creating the feelings or the other way round. However I have this need to go out and do something to take this feeling away. I really don't want to be feeling what I am feeling. I know that shopping will take my mind off things. But shopping can only do so much. Perhaps I should go for a spa day and pamper myself. Maybe that will take the feeling away. I am just not that sure that any of this will have any lasting effect. I keep going to the shops, the beauty spas, the lunches etc and for a short while it takes my mind off things and I feel great. Then the old feelings come back...

I wonder if you have thought about the concept that we live in two worlds. Simultaneously each and every minute, we live in two worlds. In other words we live "parallel" lives! This may sound like a bizarre idea, but let's explore it together.

The one world, the world that we are aware of, is the outside world. This is the world that you can see, hear, touch, smell and taste. We experience this world through our five senses. This is the world that is governed by Newtonian science. It is governed by the "what goes up must come down principals". It is predictable. It is inflexible. When we throw something up, it will always come down at the same rate and speed. If we throw a ball up in the air, it doesn't sometimes think "I might stay here a little longer today!" It will always come down at the same speed depending on the force that it was thrown and weight it carries. We can work out where the tides will be on any beach on any day and go on that day and find out that we were right. It is all science. As long as the variables stay the same, we can predict the outcomes accurately.

This is the world that we can touch. We can taste it, feel it, see it and hear it. This is the world that we can witness events and we know that those events are from the outside world because they can be experienced in that way.

At the same time we live in the inside world. This is the world of thought, of beliefs, of our values and of our dreams. This is the world of quantum physics. The world that is otherwise known as 'the world of possibility'. It is here that we can dream of things and make those dreams possible in our minds. This is the world of creation; this is where the life as we know it starts its existence. Look around … everything that you see at one time did not exist! However, it was created in someone's mind and as a result of this thought it became a tangible thing…

> *We can try things out and we can see if our mental concept will work. It is like we can have a dress rehearsal of life and see if it will work out as we think.*

This is also the world of memories. Some of the memories are from our past. Some of the memories are of our future and how we would want our future to turn out. We can remember our hopes and desires and replay them back to ourselves. We create events in our mind for our future and keep remembering them in such a way, so they become memories.

This is the world where all the events that we experience cannot be touched. They cannot be felt, heard or seen. Yet in our minds we can imagine what that touch is like, what the sounds are like, what the tastes are like and what the smells are like. And if we are not consciously aware at that moment that we are just imaging, then those thoughts feel real.

> *If we are not aware that we are just having thoughts, those same thoughts that seem real to us actually have a physical manifestation in our bodies.*

We can think of things in the past and remember them as if we are experiencing them today feeling the same feelings as we did during the original experience. For the same token, we can think of things in the future and have the feeling of excitement for a holiday or anxiety for an awkward meeting.

The past is gone and the only thing that exists is a memory of it. The thoughts that we have about our past are not real and yet we feel real emotions about them. Likewise, the thoughts that we have for the future are just as unreal. No one has knowledge of the future, so no thought about the future can be real. Yet, once again, the thought feels real and thus we feel the emotions that we have for those events.

The reason for this is because our brain is not wired in a way that can tell the difference between imagination and reality. Every thought that we have in the inside world as well as any experience that we have in the outside world, is treated in the same way.

So in the outside world right now you are reading this passage from my book. However, if you find this passage boring, in the inside world you may wander off and go and do something different. Eventually you will realize that you have wandered off and you will have to re-read the page.

Each and every moment we live in our two worlds, sometimes living them simultaneously and yet independently of each other. For example, you may be driving your car in the outside world whilst in the inside you are planning your holiday! Remember that feeling of arriving at your destination and yet you can't remember how you got there!

At the same time consider that you do everything twice!

When you get up in the morning do you go straight to the cupboard and just take out the first items you put your hands on and hope that they will match? I know that as you reading this, you may feel that some people do! What happens is that we think to ourselves about what day we are going to have and decide what clothes we want to wear. We create images and decide what will look good and get those clothes out and put them on.

Remember the feeling when you go in to the cupboard and an item of clothing that you want is not available! For a few moments, you don't know what to wear. You have to do the mental picture again. This thought process happens faster than what we can become aware of. Everything in life you do twice, you think it and then you do it.

Everything that exists in this world was a thought first. This world did not have chairs until somebody thought about them. Maybe they saw a rock that was comfortable to sit on and thought: 'if they could make some more rocks like that they could all sit down'.

All our innovations and inventions happen on the inside first for this is the world of creation; this is where the life as we know it starts its existence.

Look around … everything that you see at one time did not exist! However it was created in someone's mind and as a result of this thought it became a tangible thing … Take a look around the room you are in. Notice all the furniture, the decorations and trimmings. None of these things existed until someone thought about them. Everything that we have in the outside was first created on the inside world. Part of the world you live in, was created from your thoughts. The other parts are from other people's thoughts, so the only control you have over those parts, is how you choose to feel about those events.

More often than not, you are not consciously aware of what you are thinking before you do something. You have probably done it so many times before that it feels automatic, but if your brain doesn't tell your body what to do, it cannot do it. To tell it what to do it has to have an internal picture of what that actually looks like. Our internal pictures are known as internal representations. An internal representation is our mental pictures that sometimes are movies and sometimes they are photographs. Sometimes they are in black and white and sometimes they are in colour.

Every action you take is first a thought, as the brain cannot tell the difference between fantasy and reality, it treats both experiences the same.

In conclusion, you do everything twice. The first time you do an action, it's in the inside world and then you do the action in the outside world. When you are born you don't have many internal references, so the environment stimulates your thinking. There comes a point where the outside world becomes predictable and so does not stimulate your thoughts as before. This is where we can begin to change what is around us; we can improve our surroundings; we can create thoughts to change our environment … if we choose.

How do we do that? Firstly we need to start realizing what we are thinking about and ask ourselves about the validity of those thoughts.

Secondly, it means that we need to ask ourselves where our problems lie. If they are in the inside world, we need to deal with our inner thoughts and feelings. If they lie with the outside world then we need to deal with them with practical solutions. There is no point if we feel sad, depressed or lacking confidence going shopping. No amount of handbags, cars, shoes etc will take that feeling away. We may have temporary relief but the next morning the feelings are still there. For the same token, if you have a flat tyre, you can't meditate it back to full blown! You need to physically call a mechanic to come and repair your tyre.

Then you need to look around your world and ask yourself what part of your thinking has created your reality, and what were you thinking on the inside that created what you have got on the outside?

I know that even at work, when I am feeling nervous, I just go out and buy something. Sometimes I might go for a snack. Anything as long as the feelings go away. I wish I knew how to make the feelings stay away, so I wouldn't need to go and keep buying bags and shoes, and having facials and lunches. I wish I could feel calm and relaxed and have no need to disturb the silence and peace. Maybe if I dealt with my problems rather than running away from them! If I just fixed what is not right, in the right place, then maybe the problem can go away and stay away. The more I think of that the more I am convinced that it could work. I need to fix what is wrong inside of me, with myself, not with things from the retail world. Common sense tells me that a handbag as nice as it can be, will not make me feel the good feelings I want to feel. I am the creator of my world, and so I step into the world that is mine and sort me out ... gently!

Exercise for you:

1. Think of a problem that you are experiencing at the moment.

2. Is it in the outside world or is it in the inside world?

3. Now that you know where the problem exists, what options are available to you?

Guru: Do you remember your last day of college?

Student: Sort of … not really.

Guru: What were you wearing?

Student: My school uniform, but it was all torn and written on. School friends had written wishes of good luck all over my uniform.

Guru: What sounds can you remember?

Student: Lots of laughing, and singing. We were singing all sorts of school song and just simple happy sounds from all of us.

Guru: How did you feel?

Student: Almost dizzy, so elated, so happy, just really excited, but for what I don't know. None of us knew. There was this big world and we were going to conquer it.

Guru: What did you eat or drink that day?

Student: Ha, lots of rubbish. We were having parties all over the place. We drank lots of cheap wine and beer, homemade Bailey's and junk food, like burger with chips, crisps, chocolates. Anything that was not good for us. Oily stuff!!

Guru: What smell can you remember?

Student: Chlorine, we went swimming, so that is smell that comes to mind more than anything!

Guru: It seems to me like you actually remember quite a bit!

Student: Mmm, you are right, though I didn't think so at the start!

Chapter Two - Our Five Senses

In this chapter you will learn:

1. How we experience the outside world.
2. How our senses influence our thinking.
3. How we can use this information to enhance our lives.
4. How this helps us build rapport.

In this chapter you will be able to answer the following questions:

1. How do I know what sense I am accessing?

2. Why is it important to understand this principal?

3. How else can this knowledge help me?

4. How do I address a large audience?

I am not an artist, though I am told that I am a musician. I am good at auditory things, so it must be true. My friend is very kinaesthetic which means that he has lots of feelings. That is why he is a good friend. I am not sure if I am a good friend. Are auditory people good friends? This is all so confusing. I like drawing but I am not sure that what I am drawing is any good ... because I am not visual. I wish I was visual so that I can draw better and kinaesthetic so that I can be a good friend ...

What have you learned so far?

So far you have learned that we live in two worlds and that there is a difference in how we experience the two worlds. You have learned to identify where our problems are and to solve them from that place!

We experience the outside world through our five senses. We see things, hear them, feel them, smell them and taste them. We learn all the time through our senses. No experience happens any other way. These experiences are stored in our neurology again through our five senses. So we remember our memories through our internal seeing, hearing, feeling, tasting and smelling. The same senses are used to recall information internally.

We also invent things through our senses. When we rehearse events in the future, we imagine them in pictures, we have conversation with people in our heads, and we can feel certain sensations from our imagined experiences. Sometimes our inventions are about goals that we have and that we want to achieve for ourselves in the future.

Everything that you see around you was once a thought before it became a reality. So it would be fair to say that before reality can happen, we first have to have the experience of that event in our imaginations. In the same token that is where we are able to solve the mysteries of the mind through the language. The only way that we can translate the experiences of the inside world, is through the language that we have been taught, in the outside world.

A universal fact is that, irrespective of what physical language we use to communicate with each other, the language of our neurology … or if you like our brain is the same for all people.

The brain will process information from the outside either from what has been seen, what has been heard, what has been felt, what has been smelled and what has been tasted.

So I think that it is now a more obvious fact that we experience life through our five senses and represent them to ourselves again and again in those five senses.

It has always been that way. So this information is not new, rather it has been awakened in you.

It means that you can start to notice how you experience your world and how you make up your experiences in the outside world and the inside world. All people do this. And as you think about this, you now start to realize that this is the process that we all use in order have a living experience.

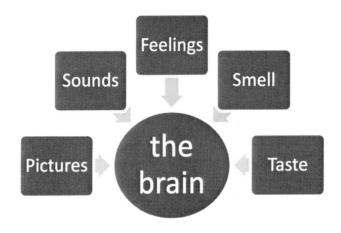

Figure 1: We experience the outside world through our five senses

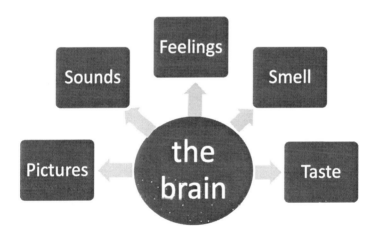

Figure 2: We create a world from inside to out

As we have our experiences in the outside world we filter them into our inside world. It would be impossible to absorb every miniscule detail of what we experience. So we have a very natural and effective filtering system (more in chapter 5).

So let's look at what happens when we have these experiences in the outside world? How is it that our experiences can get translated into our neurology?

Our system is sophisticated to say the least... and any knowing that we have is only but a mere drop in the ocean.

Having said that, there are some facts that we do know and they have been scientifically proven and those facts helps us understand the theories. This understanding will help you become an elegant and effective communicator, both at home and in your career.

We don't only use our senses to experience the world, we also use our senses to organize, store and attach meaning to our experiences from our world.

In order for us to start to understand the process of our behaviour we need to slow down the steps of that behaviour. Our brain works faster than anything that we can possibly comprehend, although we can understand and accept this fact. So by slowing the process down, we are able to take our hardwired regular routines that seems automatic and unconscious to a speed that allows us to unpick and understand them in order to be able to make relevant changes.

Remember we said that we experience our outside world through our senses. We also mentioned that we recall our experiences internally through our senses. Our five senses are otherwise referred to as our representational systems. For each of the senses there are sub-senses (chapter 3) or sub units that have finer characteristics.

When we recall an experience, we say we represent internally. The word present means to show. When we re-present, the "re" says that we are showing again. As it is internally that means it is in our inside world. In other words, to internally represent means to show ourselves again inside our minds something that we have experienced before.

An experience is represented, coded and stored through the senses and sub-senses. Of the five senses that we have, we use our visual, auditory and kinaesthetic senses the most. Although we use all of them, we tend to unconsciously favour one above the others for that experience. This will depend upon the circumstances.

> *However, to label ourselves by our favourite sense would be a mistake, as our senses change depending on internal and external influences, as well as the meaning that we have given to different events.*

For example, people can make clear mental images and think mainly in pictures, others find this difficult and may choose to talk to themselves or base their actions on a feel for the situation.

So although we all do the same thing, i.e. choose a sense to represent something to ourselves, what is different from one person to another is which sense they are using and more specifically the differences in the sub senses. It becomes an obvious observation that we do not all think in the same way.

Furthermore, when Bandler and Grinder (co founders of NLP) modelled people's behaviour, they observed that memories happened in a specific sequence. They called these strategies which is part of our programming or our scripts of life. These strategies were in a sequence of their senses. This helped them in changing strategies or streamlining them.

The other thing that they observed in people was that in speech they used words to match those representational systems. When those words were matched back, they created a much deeper rapport.

So when speaking to someone, pay attention to the words they use as this will give you a clue as to what sense they are using. If you match those worlds, you will notice that your communication rapport will be much better.

Example:

Client: I saw an advert in the newspaper of your new cars and I thought I would come and take a look. (Visual)

Salesman: Allow me to show you what we have. Any particular model and colour in mind? (Visual response)

When speaking to large audiences, you will want to use a mixture of words that contain all the senses so that you are able to match your different audiences and maximize your effectiveness.

Example:

From the things I have *seen* and from what you have *told* me, I *feel* that this is the team I want to lead! It is *clear* to me that we are on the same page, *moving forward* and *speaking* the same language.

When we use good communication, we are able to become elegantly more persuasive and influential as people can see that they can feel safe to trust us. Trust is one of the most important components in any relationship, whether in business or personal.

Below are some words for the senses.

Visual Words (See)

Observe, hazy, see, look, imagine, demonstrate, show appear, focus, portray, scan, examine, picture, notice, view, idea, glimpse, obvious.

Sound Words (Hear)

Tell, talk, discuss, heard, speak, discuss, gossip, noise, aloud, tone, listen, vocal, silent, utter, announce, earshot, call, chat, shout, sound.

Emotional Words (Feel)

Feel, gut feeling, tension, hold, grip, touch, take, fall, worry, stress, pressure, intuition, cold, hot, sensitive, stir, sore.

... and a little voice said ... "You are none of things, but you use them all!" All? I asked. Yes, all! Sometimes you will use more of your visual senses because you are drawing or doing something similar. Other times you are being a kind friend, who I know you are, so you are kinaesthetic at that moment, and sometimes when you play your violin you are using more of your auditory skills and that is why you are so good at playing the violin. You use all those things and sometimes you are using all of those at the same time.

Can that be? I asked. Yes, of course, you have a very powerful mind. It is like a sophisticated computer, only better. Let there be no limit to what you can do. Just believe in your super powers and all will be just fine.

Exercise for you:

1. Engage in conversation with someone.
2. Notice what sense they are mainly using to tell their story.
3. Match their sense by using words from the same sense.

Keep practicing till you are able to track people and match them in their speech.

You can also do this with emails.

1. Write a reply
2. Before you press send, check back on the email that you received, and now match your response by using the same words to match their sense.
3. Watch to see if you received a quicker or clearer response as a result.

Our Five Senses

Guru: I know that you have some unpleasant memories in your life. Pick one.

Student: Ok, got one.

Guru: When you imagine it in your mind, is it in colour or black and white? Is it big or is it small? Far away or close?

Student: I had not thought about it before … Colour and very near and very big … too big!

Guru: Are you in the picture or are you looking at it like an observer? Is it moving or is it still?

Student: I am in it and it is moving

Guru: What sounds are there?

Students: The sounds of that situation

Guru: Are they coming from you to the picture or from the picture to you?

Student: From the picture.

Guru: Are those sounds coming from the left, right or centre?

Student: From the left

Guru: As you experience this again inside, how do you feel?

Student: Stressed

Guru: How do you do that?

Student: I tense my jaw, my neck and shoulders, I breathe shallow and have an anticlockwise feeling moving in my stomach.

Guru: Make the picture smaller, put some distance to it, turn off the sound, soften your muscles and stop the turning in your stomach. How do you feel?

Student: mmm? What happened, what did you do? It feels different! It feels good.

Chapter Three - Our Sub Senses

In this chapter you will learn:

1. What the sub sections of our senses are.
2. How you can manipulate them to give you a more positive outcome.
3. How to match sub senses with others to build strong rapport.

In this chapter you will be able to answer the following questions:

1. Why do some thoughts feel more powerful than others?
2. How do I know what will be the most effective change to make?
3. Will this be a permanent change?
4. What do I need to notice to enhance rapport building?

I feel overwhelmed. Everything is coming down on me and I feel so much 'overwhelm'. I need some distance from my situation, some different perspective. If only I could stop thinking of this situation, I think I might have some relief ... but I can't, my thoughts just keep going round and round. I keep thinking of the same thing. It feels like that is all I think about! I can see my thoughts clearly and hear the sounds ... it all makes me feel so overwhelmed. I can't move or act on this ... but I know I must, just wish I could get some distance, so that things can become clear...

What have I learnt so far?

So far you have learned that we live in two worlds and we experience our world through our five senses. Once we have had an external experience, we store it in our neurology through those five senses. When we remember those experiences again, we remember them through our five senses.

Knowing this information is a hell of a lot of "what we do" and nothing of "what is the point of it all". It is all interesting bits of information.

This is however the start of living a life that has more conscious awareness. It is through conscious awareness that we obtain power to make lasting changes to ourselves and to others. So read on and discover the importance of all of this.

It is not enough to just know what the processes are, we need to know what to do that will make a difference to our lives.

When we look at something on the outside world, we can notice shapes, colours, how near or far something is. We can also notice sounds and pick up the difference in the tone of sound, how clearly we can hear something or not. Certain things make us feel a certain way. So we can feel the outside temperature and that will either make us feel comfortable or not.

In much the same way we do the same thing in the inside world, with a few extra attributes. In the inside world, how we structure and arrange our thoughts and our sub senses represent how we structure our internal experience. Science has proven that our brain cannot tell the difference between an external or internal experience, therefore what we think, will affect the way that we see and therefore experience the outside world.

Our view of the world is governed by how we think of ourselves and how we see the world through the filter of our thoughts.

It affects our moment to moment thoughts as well as our beliefs and values. So when we want to do something, what we believe about our ability to do it, has to do with how we think of that situation and our relation to it.

Lets first look at the sub-section of the senses and then I will discuss what this means and how you can make changes.

Within each modality there is more detail. It is not enough to know that you can "re see" things in your mind. Now we start to get into the details of our thoughts. So when we recall a memory, what we need to do is look to understand how we represent in detail that memory to ourselves.

Each modality has sub sections, otherwise known as sub-senses. There is no right or wrong way of representing, instead *it just is*. We adopt an attitude of curiosity and search for knowledge in the process of how we do things rather than why and what history we have about it.

All sub senses have certain things in common. These attributes are there for all of us; however what we want to establish is how specifically we create any particular thought. Any thought will have the following visual sub senses: There will be a location, in other words where you place any particular thought. For example, the distance from us, is it near or far? Size, is it big or small? Clarity, is it clear or hazy? Are you in the picture or are you watching as if you are watching a movie of yourself? Is it in colour or black and white? Is it moving like a movie or is it still like a photograph?

So think of anything from your past and ask yourself, where do you feel the thought is? Is it to your right or left or perhaps in the centre? Do you see your memory in colour or black and white? Is it big or is it small? Is it near you or is far away? Do you see the memory through your eyes or do you see yourself in the picture? Is the memory like a movie or is like a still photograph? Is it clear or is hazy?

For the auditory attributes you ask yourselves, where is the sound, is it coming from the outside in or from your head out? Is it your voice or is someone else's? What is the tone like, harsh or gentle? Is it loud or soft?

As you think of your memory, think of the sounds that go with it. Sometimes there is silence, in which case you will ask yourself is this silence inside of you or it outside? If you hear sounds, are they clear? Do you hear words or is it general sounds? Are they loud or soft and far away or close? What is the tone of the sound? What emotion can you feel as you hear them?

For the kinaesthetic attributes you ask yourselves, what feeling do I get with that memory? Where is the feeling located? It will be in one of four places, the stomach, solar plexus, chest and occasionally it might be felt in the face. But think of this logically! If the feeling is of tightness from stress, it won't be felt first in your knee. So get curious without judgement and simply notice where you first feel a feeling that is associated with your memory! Play around to discover where you feel your feelings.

In our torsos we have our enteric nervous system which governs our feelings in that area. Our brain communicates to the enteric system through the spine. So when we have thoughts, the meaning that we have given to those thoughts travel to our enteric system through the spine. That is why we feel those feelings in our torso.

These feelings typically will have four ways of moving. They either go clockwise or anticlockwise or they spin outwards or inwards. Again think of a

54

memory and ask yourself where do I feel the feeling? Is it in my stomach, my solar plexus, my chest or my face? How is this feeling moving? If you are not sure, then just try replicating the movement with your hands and you will soon feel the direction that is right. Again there is no right or wrong, just an observation of what is.

And of course we do have the taste and smell senses so in some cases we will observe the subsection of those senses. For smell, we will ask ourselves what is that we can smell and what is the relation to the memory? For taste, what can we taste, and again how does this relate to the memory?

How can we use this information to help us make changes? So far you have learned that you created your memories in a particular way. This process is all unconsciously done and learned by the method of modelling your behaviour from others.

We learn to live life through our parent's example, other people's way of living. We live our life by the paradigms of others.

If some of those paradigms don't serve your life, you need to observe what works and what doesn't and make changes. Up until now you never questioned if what you are thinking is to your benefit or your detriment. You unconsciously created and arranged your thoughts in a particular way from your observations.

Now is the time to step back and ask yourselves is this useful to me and if not what can you do to change it? How do I change the order and the attributes of my memories in order to create a different association that will have a different feeling for me? Once you have observed the properties of the memory that doesn't serve you and have worked out what sub senses you have attached to them, you can start to mess with them. Literally mess them up.

If something is near to you, it will feel more important. Think of it from a logical perspective. The closer we are to something the more we can see, hear and feel it. With your thoughts you have the same experience, except they are internal.

So now try to put some distance between you and that thought. Notice all along how you feel, does the feeling stay the same, is it better or worse. If better, then leave it there and continue to try something else. This time change the size of it and again notice how it feels. Is it the same, better or worse? If it feels worse put back to the way it was. Make clear pictures hazy; take them from the left to the right; from up to down and from colour to black and white.

Change the sounds by making them softer, make the words slower, change the accents or the tone, so they sound different and feel different as a result.

Use your imagination to make whatever changes you want to make. After all it is your mind so put no limit to improving your thoughts so that you can have a better quality of life.

One of the most key advantages to understanding your thoughts is to improve your own internal interpretation of the world. If you have given an event in your life a negative meaning and as a result you feel bad, it is time now for you to ask yourself if you want to keep feeling this way or do you want to change. You can't change the past, for it is gone and not accessible, the one thing about it that you can change is how you think about it and as a result how you feel about it.

How you feel about it comes down to what meaning you have given to it. As you become the observer of your life and your thoughts, you can stand back and ask yourself: "how can I change my thoughts so that I can feel different?" The surprising thing is that you don't have to be philosophical about it. It is a romantic idea that if you understood your past it would help you release thoughts and feelings that make you feel bad about yourself. However, in my own personal experience and my experience in working with others, this has never proven to be the case.

If anything, the more information about the past that can't be changed the more it causes anger, confusion, feelings of rejection, shame and worthlessness. It has been more useful to understand what we do and how we do it and then change the process rather than to have an understanding of why we feel the way we do. The process of our thoughts is what makes us feel good, indifferent or bad about an event.

We have a very precise process of arranging all our memories ... past or future ones. It is a very simplistic idea that makes a big difference to one's life. Despite the simplicity of it, it should not be underestimated.

When we have thoughts that are large, near to us and very clear, they will feel stronger and more intense than those thoughts that are small, far away and hazy. The clearer the picture the more powerful the thoughts feel.

Think of the last time you were at the cinema. The movie screen is big, close by and very clear! Together with good sound effects, a movie when presented in this way will easily induce certain feelings in you. What if the screen was small, you sat very far away and it was blurry or hazy with bad muffled sound? Would the movie be something that you would enjoy and pay attention to? No! You would ask for your money back. With our thoughts it is similar. It does not matter if you are making good movies about your future or remembering good movies from the past or whether you are making horror movies about future events or remembering bad episodes! The clearer you make them, the nearer they are in your mind the bigger the intensity in our feeling ... good or bad. So if a thought makes you feel bad, change the properties so that the values are diminished and the feeling changes to indifference or apathy.

> *Negative thoughts can prevent us from doing the things that we want to do. They can make us procrastinate, not do well in test or exams and make bad speeches etc.*

So when we are able to take control of the thought and change the association it will have a positive and significant impact on our life.

The most common question I get is *what should I change that will make the most difference?* The answer is "I don't know!" For each person and then for each thought there will always be a driver. A driver is that part of the thought that will make the most difference if changed. For some thoughts, if the sound and the tone changes, the thought changes. For other's it might be the distance or the size, or changing the direction of the way that the feelings are spinning. The best advice to give you is to notice, be tenacious and keep going till you find the driver that makes the biggest difference for you to that thought. Conscious awareness is the start.

Observe yourself and the way you create your thoughts and then ask yourself ..."do I want to continue to think this way and feel this way?"

If not, make the effort to change. Feeling positive makes you more resilient and more likely to make permanent changes. Bad states or emotions interfere with our problem solving ability. We cannot solve our problems in the same mental state that created them in the first place.

Our brain is funny a thing and the way and the reason we hold on to things can be equally confusing. We learn faster than anything that we can understand. Sometimes with one go, change is permanent. Having said that, sometimes we need to be more persistent and have to make the changes several times for it to be permanent. Whatever works. Be tenacious and never give up.

Sometimes we need to combine this skill with other techniques that will be mentioned later on in the book. Again, I will say this to you: decide to become the observer and the ruler of your life and your mind and, with that, take control about what you absorb and how you view the world. Accept that you are responsible for your life's outcomes. With this acceptance comes power to change.

> *While the world holds the reasons of why your life is the way it is, you are powerless to make the changes you want.*

The other big advantage is that through listening to the language that is used to describe events we are able to hear the other people's senses and sub senses. Together with matching the senses you can now conversationally begin to create a feeling of deep understanding between you and the speaker which helps build rapport quicker and stronger.

As we have already said, rapport builds trust which means that they will offer information that you have not asked for. In any conversation, the minute someone offers more information than you asked for, that is a sure sign that you have established rapport and the speaker trusts you. This skill in relationship building, whether professionally or personally, is a very valuable tool. On the next page is a table that you can use to elicit the sub senses of different experiences and then you can compare the differences.

You could compare a thought that you find simple to a thought that you find confusing. Or compare what you think is difficult to what you think is easy. You are looking for the properties and not the content because you are looking for the process, this is also useful if you are doing this exercise with someone else and it is not appropriate to share the content.

Sub-senses comparison

Visual	Experience	Experience
Location of image		
Movie or photo		
Colour or black and white		
Bright/dark		
Clear/hazy		
Floating or with edges		
are you in it /are you watching yourself		
Big/small		
Shape		
3d2d		
Close/Far		
Sound		
What sound		
Volume		
Tonality		
Speed of sound		
Yours /someone else's		

from you/towards you		
Emotions		
Where in body		
Breath speed		
Heart rate		
Hot/cold		
Heavy/light		
Smooth/rough		
High emotion/low emotion		
Type of touch		
Smell and Taste		
Type of smell		
Familiar/unfamiliar		
Is the taste pleasant or unpleasant		

...if things became clear I would feel better. I am told to observe! How do I observe me, my thoughts? How do I step back and do that? I am to just take my thought and put it in front of me and just look at it ... as if it not mine, as if someone else's. And when I do that ... I notice that what I am observing is sad, however when I push it away from me, it mysteriously feels less intense. If I turn the sound off, my thought feels as if it is unimportant right now. I put more distance and change it from left to right. Now I really feel nothing. Plain nothing. It feels as if I am watching an old black and white movie with no titles, no music and therefore no feelings. I observe and decide as the observer and master of my mind, this is not important for me to give it any feeling, any thought or any importance. I let it go, easily. Peace at last...

Exercise for you:

1. Think of an event that causes you to feel uncomfortable.
2. Identify exactly what the feeling is that you have.
3. Ask yourself what you would rather feel in its place.
4. Notice the properties from all the sub senses that it has.
5. Start one by one to change them and notice with each change what you are feeling.
6. Ask yourself if you are feeling the same, better or worse.
7. Keep going till you are able to change the feeling to what you want it to be.

Guru: The most important thing in your life is what you decide is important!

Student: And why is that?

Guru: Because when we make something important we put more emphasis on it and exaggerate the event and so it can feel more important.

Student: Is that bad?

Guru: It is neither. *It just is!* You need to ask yourself the question: is the result that I have the result that I want?

Student: Do you mean that if my result is one of anger, I need to ask myself "Do I want to be angry?"

Guru: Yes and does the anger serve to get me the best outcome.

Student: But sometimes I am right, can I then be angry?

Guru: If that is what you choose! Right or wrong, getting angry happens in your body and no one else's. Is that what you want?

Student: Is there any harm to that?

Guru: Think of how your body reacts when you get angry. How is your muscle tone, your breathing and your ability to think creatively and strategically? Is that what you want?

Student: Well no, anger does not make me feel good at all, but I never saw it as a choice. It just happens!

Guru: Nothing just happens. Everything we are and everything we feel, we do intentionally, but we have so fine-tuned our ability to do the things that we do, they feel automatic.

Chapter Four - Brain Juice

In this chapter you will learn:

1. How thoughts transfer to the body.
2. How to identify the different types of brain juice.
3. What does this mean to us.

In this chapter you will be able to answer the following questions:

1. What type of brain juice am I making?
2. What does this mean?
3. What does this stop me doing?
4. How can I change the type of brain juice?

I can't breathe. I feel like my chest is going to explode. My chest is tight with tension. I keep thinking of my business and all the 'what ifs'! What if I can't get the next contract? What if my client does not pay me? How am I going to support my family? I am supposed to look after them and I won't be able to! What am I supposed to do? The stress is making me so tired ... I can't think straight, I can't do my job, all I keep thinking is what will happen if I don't succeed! I feel like I am drowning in my worries...

What have I learned so far?

So far you have learned that we live in two worlds and we experience our world through our five senses. Once we have had an external experience, we store it in our neurology through those five senses. When we remember those experiences again, we remember them through our five senses. To better understand our thoughts we looked at the sub sections of our five senses, as this revealed our process for that particular behaviour.

By changing parts of the process, we are able to change the way we create that thought, which in turn changes the way we feel about that thought and ultimately the connection we have to that subject. We can reprogram ourselves to feel differently by becoming consciously aware and making changes to our life long programmes.

 Knowing this information is a hell of a lot of "what we do" and nothing of "what is the point of it all". It is all interesting bits of information.

This is however the start of living a life that has more conscious awareness. It is through conscious awareness that we obtain power to make lasting changes to ourselves and to others.

In the inside world, how we structure and arrange our thoughts and our sub senses represent how we structure our internal experience. Science has proven that our brain cannot tell the difference between an external or internal experience, therefore what think, will affect the way that we see and therefore experience the outside world.

> *Our view of the world is governed by how we think of ourselves and how we see the world through the filter of our thoughts.*

It affects our moment to moment thoughts as well as our beliefs and values. So when we want to do something, what we believe about our ability to do it, has to do with how we think of that situation and our relation to it.

To better understand our thoughts we look at the sub sections of our five senses as this reveals our process for that particular behaviour. By changing parts of the process we are able to change the way we create that thought which in turn changes the way we feel about that thought and ultimately the connection we have to that subject. We can reprogram ourselves to feel differently by becoming consciously aware and making changes to our life long programmes.

I want you to imagine that someone is walking down the road. Suddenly they jump up in fright! Although we may not be able to read their mind, we know that something or someone must have frightened them. It is logical for us to think that we are not simply creatures that experience emotions randomly.

> *We are very precise in our strategies, so everything that we do is intentional.*

A healthy body does not have the ability to act randomly and without reason. As long as we are physically healthy our bodies will act with purpose and intention. We are very sophisticated animals, with an intelligence that we ourselves don't fully understand and appreciate.

Science now claims that we have between 60,000 to 80,000 thoughts a day. Here is a sad fact ... most of those thoughts are the same thoughts that we had yesterday and the day before. Every now and then we make one of those thoughts important. The only way that a thought can be felt or measured by ourselves is through feeling. So there has to be a way that a thought gets to be translated into the body and that way is through our internal chemistry.

This is how thoughts communicate to the body so that the body will know what to do. It is the universal language of the mind. Our mind and body are connected. We have a sophisticated system that works together to provide a way that thoughts can become feelings and actions. That is the very basis of our behaviour. So our every thought that we decide is important will create a chemical that will go to our body.

When thoughts are made important, they are translated into chemicals that travel to every cell and organ of our body.

They pass the chemical information so that we have what we call a physical manifestation. So what we see as behaviour in ourselves or others is a series of events that have happened internally faster than anything that we can comprehend. These systems are interrelated and work on more than one event simultaneously.

Now I know that the system that governs our neurology is complicated to say the least. However, on the basic level it is easy to understand. When I was studying NLP with Dr Richard Bandler and John La Valle, John referred to these chemicals as Brain Juice. It is a simple term to explain a very complicated process. After all we are not neuroscientist.

Every thought will create its own biochemical reaction in the brain. In simple terms your thoughts, when made important so that we notice them, create brain juice.

Brain juice is the cocktail of chemical messengers of our thoughts which the brain will release into the body. Brain juice is our thought messengers. We have receptors in every cell and they are able to receive the information that the messengers carry to the cells within the body.

There is a down side to our unconscious mind. It does not have the ability to judge and differentiate between good and bad. Remember that things *just are*! What makes an event good or bad is what we decide to label it as according to the values and beliefs we have.

Depending on what we have labelled something will determine what type of brain juice will be created. Our unconscious mind is simply the obedient messenger. This allows the body to react in accordance to the thoughts generated.

This is where personal awareness starts to work in our favour. Let's imagine that we can divide brain juice in two major categories. There would be bad brain juice and good brain juice.

> *The easiest way to realise the type of "brain juice" is to ask, "What am I feeling right now?" Am I feeling comfortable or uncomfortable?*

All emotions can be identified by whether you feel good or bad. Below is a list of good and brain juice for you to see:

Good Brain Juice:

Success, Love, Freedom, contribution, pride, comfort, passion, joy, intimacy, relaxation, confidence, adventure, fun, security.

Bad Brain Juice:

Anger, stress, guilt, fear, frustration, rejection, depression, anxiety, worthlessness, hopelessness, helplessness.

In a very simple way the different type of chemicals that we create are easily identified. They are either good or bad. So what does that mean to us?

Think of when you make good brain juice! How do you feel? When you fall in love, don't you feel invincible? Do you feel you can overcome everything! That you are creative and can come up with wonderful ideas? Good brain juice helps you stay resilient in bad times.

> *Resilient people recover quicker from stress and have more flexibility to adapt to circumstances making them more likely to succeed.*

Think about how you feel when you make bad brain juice! Do you feel good? Are you able to breathe well? Are you able to think well? Do you feel energised? Can you get a good night's sleep?

You are able to easily identify what type of brain juice you are making by simply asking yourself how you are feeling!

There are instances in life where you are angry, sad, anxious etc., and in your mind you can justify it! You are right! Someone has done you an injustice. However those chemicals that create those states are the chemicals your body makes in you.

> *No one but you is experiencing the physical manifestation of your bad brain juice.*

No one suffers the tension in your muscles or the lack of oxygen in your blood or the tiredness that comes from stress except for you. Is there anything or anyone that is worth your mental state and more importantly your health?

Think of times when you experienced bad brain juice, and as a result what were you not able to do? Teenagers in school often forget information that they have learned for exams, only to remember it once the exam is over and they have relaxed and started to breathe properly as a result of relaxing. Equally, adults forget their speeches, feel awkward during meetings and do not communicate clearly etc. Bad brain juice does not enhance your life; rather it takes feeling good and living happy away from you.

What could possibly be more important than your own health? All the money in the world, all the success and fame are worth nothing if you are sick and can't enjoy them.

Science has proven that stress is one of the main reasons for a weak immune system and this can lead to diseases in the body. During times of adversity you are more prone to illness unless you are consciously aware of your state and you consciously choose to do something about it.

Doctors will advise patients that suffer with depression to exercise. Exercise will create endorphins and serotonin which are 'feel-good' chemicals. But more than that, exercising the body is a different state to the depressed state and so it forces the body to make chemicals that are good!

Sometimes we may not feel like going for a walk, we may not want to have a swim or ride a bike. But in time of stress when the body is fighting and is feeling tired, exercise is not a choice, it is a must! The exercise forces us to breathe better which oxygenates the blood, it forces the brain to make good brain juice and as a result we begin to feel better and with that we get better. We are again able to think clearly and make good decisions and be more creative.

Basically, good or bad brain juice comes down to how you are feeling physically and what your muscle tone is. In turn this affects your circulation and how you are breathing, which affects the level of oxygen in your blood. We may think of it from a point of emotions, but it is all just chemistry! *It just is.*

... what did they say ... I can't remember ... aaah yes, to breathe, just breathe ... start with that, then walk, go for walks, meditate! Create intentionally good chemicals in my body so I can help my body become more resourceful. It feels hard at first, for I naturally want to keep doing what I have always done. I have to re-teach my mind to do something different because it governs my body and I want to change the way I behave, I want to stop the stresses of my life. I understand that to change my life, I need to change my life. Which means that I need to change the things I am doing now in my life? I need to change the negative thoughts so that I can bring about change. Every morning, I will take time to reflect on my life. I will become consciously aware of my thoughts and if they are ones that create bad emotions, then I will consciously change those feelings. To help my body and to influence my mind, to think in ways that are more resourceful rather than detrimental to me. I make this promise to myself...

Exercise for you:

1. Think of a time that you felt unresourceful.
2. Ask yourself, if you could choose any feeling, would you still choose this one?
3. If yes, what is the benefit of this emotion for you right now?
4. If not, what feeling would you rather choose?
5. Choose consciously for yourself to feel the positive feeling for this moment.

Guru: Inside your mind you have an internal system that guides your behaviour and therefore your outcomes.

Student: What like a map?

Guru: Yes, kind of. It helps your unconscious know where the start and end of a particular behaviour is. Think of your behaviours, they all have a beginning and an end, don't they?

Student: I understand ... kind of, but not sure how this is fits in with my life.

Guru: If your map of the world says that public speaking is scary then you will feel scared to give public speeches. Your maps are your programs and they guide you.

Student: Would that be wrong?

Guru: Only if you need to give public talks. If the map takes you to a destination that you don't want, that map is no good to you.

Student: How did I create the map?

Guru: You copied them from those around you.

Student: So if I copied maps that work in my life, then that is good, however if I copied maps that don't give me the result that I want then that is not so good.

Guru: The tube map of London is good if you are going on the tube, but not if you are walking around London. In the same way, the maps of your behaviour may be ok in some instances, but not in others. Your personal awareness will help you gauge if your maps are working for you or not!

Chapter Five – We create maps

In this chapter you will learn:

1. how we create the maps
2. how your behaviours are automated
3. why you keep doing the same behaviour
4. how to make changes in our maps

In this chapter you will be able to answer the following questions:

1. Why do certain situations make me feel a certain way?
2. Are my maps the same as others?
3. Does my map mean anything about me?
4. Is my map real?

I am sure I am right! I am sure what I remember is the way things happened! I have not made things up. I am very good at remembering even the tiniest detail. And I do think that I am fair and unbiased. Yet, to myself I can admit that there some things that I don't remember that clearly ... they are not important, so it does not matter. What I do remember is right, so I believe I am right! Why are they all still arguing with me? Why can't they see my point of view! Why don't they understand me? What is wrong with them? Are they stupid? It can be so frustrating when people don't get you!

What have I learnt so far?

So far you have learned that we live in two worlds and we experience our world through our five senses. Once we have had an external experience, we store it in our neurology through those five senses. When we remember those experiences again, we remember them through our five senses. To better understand our thoughts we looked at the sub sections of our five senses, as this revealed our process for that particular behaviour.

By changing parts of the process, we are able to change the way we create that thought, which in turn changes the way we feel about that thought and ultimately the connection we have to that subject. We can reprogram ourselves to feel differently by becoming consciously aware and making changes to our life long programmes.

We have also learned that all our thoughts get translated into the body through the chemicals that we produce and this creates behaviour. To simplify, we call those chemicals brain juice and we subcategorised them into good and bad. We are able to tell what type of brain juice we are making by noticing how we feel physically. And by noticing how we feel, we can question whether it is appropriate to feel this way and make changes if necessary.

But the big question in all of us is how we create those thoughts and why is it that they make us feel a certain way? Why is it that some experiences make us feel glad, while others make us feel sad? In 1931, Alfred Korzybski coined the phrase "the map is not the territory" and it is still used today! It has since been quoted by many people for its metaphorical meaning that explains how we create our experiences.

Let's go back to basics. I want you to imagine that there has been an experience of sorts. It could be something that you saw, or heard, or something you felt, or perhaps something that you thought of. In order for us to store that experience we need some kind of a process. Now it is important that you understand that we all do the same process, however, it varies in degrees depending on the experience and the person. We talked about how we store with our senses. The interesting thing is that no two people do the same process in the same way. Some will store in coloured images, and some will store in black and white. Some will have moving images and some will have still. Even if two people have moving images, the speed of the moment is bound to differ.

As human beings we do the same thing, what makes us different is the detail of our process which is unique to us in every instance.

If we were to absorb everything that we experienced it would be information overload; to help avoid that, we have a very intelligent filtering system. Our unconscious mind will delete some of the information that it thinks is not important. It will distort it so it makes sense and it will generalise to make it easy to identify and learn. Once a behaviour has been made and tested it becomes a strategy. When the strategy has been working we start to believe that it works and so we will teach others to do the same. This learning is unconscious and so our behaviour feels automated. It doesn't feel as if you are creating the behaviour but rather that it is just happening to you. In order to change behaviour you first need to become aware of the automated map that you are following.

Imagine that I have a map of London in front of me. Is the map London? No, you say. It is a representation of London. It is a drawing that looks like London and represents London. For the cartographer to put London on an A4 piece of paper he had to distort the size of it. They would have to alter it so that it can fit. They make it fit. There are maps of London in all shapes and sizes. The suitability of the map will depend upon the person and what they need it for. Someone that is looking for cycle paths in London will need a different map than that of a person who is site seeing. That doesn't mean anything about the map. It just is! Whatever meaning it gets, it gets from you.

Now London looks smaller. We are intelligent enough to understand that and so we accept this fact without any argument. In the distortion process, the cartographer had to delete a lot of information and leave only what he thought was important. So now, although the map looks like London, its size is wrong and there is information that is missing ... it has become impoverished. To add to that, because of a lack of space, the cartographer also had to generalize information so that the map can function. We may see symbols for churches for example; however we don't know what type of church it is. We may see symbols for schools and not know what school is there. So as much as we accept this information we also recognise that this is not the true experience and that the map is impoverished.

We do the same things in life, we see, hear and feel events and only absorb what we think is important to us, delete some of the information, give it our own meaning from our previous experiences, beliefs, values, and generalized by linking it to something else that we have experienced that is similar. The only difference is that we don't recognise that we are doing this so the process that we create feels like the real thing. This process helps us live day by day and, for the most part it works. Sometimes though it doesn't. Sometimes these thoughts and maps make us feel not deserving, not enough, not acceptable. This is not true, but it feels that way. We create maps that have a beginning and an end. Our maps make us feel that way and because it is our new truth, we believe it. Our maps can fail us. And if we are not consciously aware of that simple fact, we don't realize it. Our maps are our subjective interpretation of the world. Subjective for it is built on our previous experiences, beliefs and values.

As much as this helps us become more efficient, it also takes away from us the real experience and what we store is no longer the true experience. The works of neuroscientist today have now proven that we all create our own perception of reality. We all have our version of what we think reality is. It is our perception. It feels true enough to us ... for after all it is our version of the real thing. Events may be similar but not the same. It now becomes our truth, our reality.

> *The madness in the world is that we all believe that our reality is the right one...*
>
> *We will defend our belief about that reality.*
>
> *And for that right we will fight!*

The mystery of behaviour lies in the way that we create the maps in our minds. When we begin to analyse the behaviour, we discover that we have a very specific way of representing the world in our minds that is unique to us. The words, sounds and things that we see, work as anchors that will trigger past experiences or events and will stimulate us to use our representational systems to store information and experience life.

One of the hardest things for any individual to do is first become aware of this process and then to realize that what we think is not the same as what it really is! And more importantly that we are possibly wrong or there could be another meaning to an event.

It is this understanding and accepting that the meaning that we have given an event has come from our interpretation and therefore it is no more than just a thought that we are having. Flexibility builds success, for those who are flexible will accept that there is more than one way to think about something and there is more than one way to do something and that it is possible that there is more than one meaning to any one event.

> *Allow yourself to comfortably be wrong and make changes that work towards a successful and comfortable life.*

The maps or models that we create will in turn produce behaviour. We build the maps first and then we use them to know what we are meant to be doing ... a bit like following a real map.

This links back to the fact that we do everything in life twice. We create it once in our minds and then again physically.

So what Korzybski was saying ("the map is not the territory") is that what we have as memories and thoughts or ideas are not what the real event was. At every moment of our life we are functioning out of our own perception of the world and although that feels like reality, it is only the reality that we have created for ourselves.

When someone gets stuck in life, they are stuck on the map and not in the territory. In other words, it is just a thought that causes the limitation. What we do with the thought will either make us feel as if we are stuck or flowing. Thoughts create behaviour. The good news is that we were not born with those behaviours, we have learned them. So if something is unresourceful we can, with conscious effort, unlearn it. It may feel uncomfortable and out of your comfort zone, however ask yourself the question *'do you want to feel uncomfortable for the rest of your life, doing what doesn't work, or uncomfortable for a short time while relearning new paradigms that you have created for your life?'*

Imagine that you are sitting in a movie theatre and the screen is blank. Every time you hear a sound or a word or have an experience, you place an image on that screen which will represent your experience. If you add more than what you have, then you know that you are using information from your past experiences. The new image on your screen is therefore not a real one but one that you have enhanced.

Your particular enhancement process could be either very resourceful or very un-resourceful. The clue to knowing which one is more resourceful depends on how you feel when you think of that experience. And how you think will determine how you feel about the experience. Is it right or is it wrong? It just is, and then you decide what you want to do with it.

We come to the understanding that when we are stuck, our problems are mapping problems. When you get stuck in the map, you feel like you have an edge where you believe that you can't step further and so you don't …chances are that you can. Don't forget that the map is inside your head and does not really exist.

We experience frustration, distress and aggravation because the "world" lacks resources and solutions. However, it is actually our map of the world where the 'lacking' is! The outside world is complete. When you step off your edge of your map, you step into a new world, one that offers different learning and so offers different experiences. To change your life, you need to change the things you are doing. New maps provide new behaviours and with that new solutions.

All 'problems' in the world are of a linguistic construction, found in our own representations of our world. No one has actually seen a 'problem' as the world is not able to represent problems. Problems are not tangible. They can't be seen, heard or touched in the outside world. In the outside world we have events. What the event means and if they become problems is because internally we decided that that is what they are. So again it is our own thought process that creates the problems that we have!

Sometimes the mind will slip into insanity and stop rationally thinking. In those moments it is the wisdom in us and not the intelligence that will protect and guide us to do the right thing and to help us decide what is real and what just a thought is.

If two people are in an argument, you may say that that is real. You can see the people arguing and you can hear it. So it is real. However, what is real is that there are two people that are not in agreement.

If that is a problem, it is because in your mind you interpret the event as a problem. What would that experience be like for you if you didn't know the people and you could not understand their language? Would it feel the same? Would it still be a problem or would it be something different?

An understanding and a realisation of this empowers one to question feelings and events rather than take them for granted.

So why do we create maps? Our maps guide our behaviour. They contain our behavioural strategies. This is how we know to do the 'right' behaviour at the right time.

All of our maps and thus all of our behaviours are started by a trigger. The process of that behaviour will run and then it will end when the criteria is met. If you think of brushing your teeth, something will prompt you to start the process. You have a strategy on how to brush your teeth and a set of criteria that tells you when to finish. If not you would be brushing your teeth all day.

So what are your triggers? If your map of the world says that presentations are scary, what are the triggers? Is it scary when you are presenting to one person or to a small group of people? Or more? Do those people have to be strangers or do they have to be your peers? When do you start being scared and how long do you stay scared for?

Conscious awareness of the fact that we create maps to function in our world, opens the door to new meaning and new possibilities. Our mapping problems can be broken down and better understood through the language that we use. Knowing that we are looking for a beginning and an end to create change empowers us to achieve the life that we want and deserve. More often than not, by realizing that the map we are using is not the map that will give us the outcome that we want is enough for us to go and find new maps and break new ground and learn new behaviours!

... if I can understand, why can't they? If I get it, why don't they? Is it that they see the world differently? Is my view of the world different? Are my beliefs different? It must be. It is the only thing that makes sense! It is about the theory that we all create our own unique perception of the world and we work out of that. So my point of view is not shared then! That makes sense! That makes perfect sense! I need to explain things in a way that they can understand, for they don't understand my world in the same way I do. No one does, only I do! It is what makes me unique. It is my uniqueness and specialness. It is everyone's! I feel like I have just woken up!

Exercise for you:

1. Think of something that you do that is not that resourceful.
2. Ask yourself; what is the trigger that you have that starts the behaviour? In other words, what has to happen for you to start to behave in a certain way?
3. What has to happen for you to stop doing that behaviour? And think of this from the angle that you do not continue with any behaviour indefinitely.
4. What is the path that you take from the start to the finish?
5. Is this what you want to keep doing? Where can you make changes?

Part Two

Gabrielle has learned it,
however she is not quite using it...
...she does not know it well enough!
If she knew it, she would use it.
We do what we know

iUnderstand Me

Introduction

In life we constantly have experiences. Those experiences as we have discussed earlier in the book are experienced through our five senses and converted into memories. Because it would be impossible to absorb every miniscule detail of that experience, the process whereby we take an experience from the outside world and store it in our minds as memory goes through a filtering system. We omit parts of the information and generalize others from what we have experienced and by doing that we alter the true experience to become our version of what we think happened. What now sits in our deep memory is our version of what the original experience was. We will be aware of some parts of it and unaware of other parts that can be retrieved from the deep memory through skilled questioning.

The reason that this happens is because the conscious mind can only process a small amount. Go into a room and have a quick glance around. Now go out of the room and write down all that you saw and notice how much detail you can remember. When you go back into the room, you will see that there are a lot of things that you had already, in a short space of time forgotten. You realize that there is more than what you wrote down. You may be thinking ... well yes that is obvious! And it is obvious, and it is what we naturally do. However, we absorb more than what we are consciously aware of as our unconscious mind can absorb a huge amount of information. Not all of it, but a greater amount.

So when people speak, what we hear is a summarized version of their deep memory that they both consciously and unconsciously remember of the experience. If we were to share every detail as we had experienced and now have as memory, a one month holiday would take one month to share with someone. So we summarize and condense our experiences when we share them with others. It helps us become more effective and efficient. However, it also helps us become equally inefficient and ineffective. The summarizing process that we all do alters the original experience and it now starts to move more and more away from the truth. It is important to understand this for it is key to understanding yourself, others, and improving working relationships.

Here is the scary part of all of this! When someone hears you speak this starts the process again. What they hear is an external experience that they will, through their unique filtering process, store in their deep memory!

You guessed it! They will leave information out; generalize parts of it and by doing so it alters the original experience, moving it more away from the truth.

What is important about this obvious piece of information is that we live our lives like this. We don't have a conscious awareness that we don't naturally remember everything. This alters our perception of reality and reduces it to what we think it is. When that happens and, it happens unconsciously to us, we start to live and build maps from our sense of reality which is different from the real experience.

From a "mapping" point of view, what we are doing is building impoverished maps! That is not always a bad thing. If your map of the world says that public speaking is an empowering and wonderful feeling that is good if you need to stand in front of a lot of people and deliver speeches. If your map of the world leaves out the part that it is empowering and a wonderful feeling and puts in that it is a scary experience, then that won't help you.

However, in our deep memory there is always more information and, so by becoming aware firstly that this process happens, we can then start to listen and notice what is missing and start to retrieve it so that the information is more accurate and more resourceful.

In part two, we focus on how we label things that cause us to stop thinking and how to start not only to listen to what is altered, generalized and omitted, but also how to retrieve information. I will also share with you how to understand what this unconscious use of language patterns tells us about the speaker's maps of that experience. All problems, limitations and lacking of self-belief can be heard through the use of these patterns, and not only can they be heard, they can be understood from a process point of view. So although we may not always understand the 'why' of a particular behaviour, we will understand the how which holds the key to change.

Guru: What do you see when you hear something?

Student: I didn't think I saw anything... I was just listening!

Guru: But for you to understand any word, your mind makes pictures. We have learned to identify utterances on the outside with pictures on the inside. If I say apple, what do you see inside your mind?

Student: An apple! That is so cool! You are right, I had never thought of that.

Guru: Most people are unaware of this process. We were not created to interpret English, Dutch, Greek or any other language. That is something that we have developed through our evolution. But our internal language is one of pictures, sounds, feelings, smells and tastes. That way we know what we have heard, for we see it inside of our minds.

The thing is, if there is information missing we will naturally fill in the gaps, otherwise things don't make sense.

Student: That is ok, isn't it?

Guru: Well what you fill them in with is your stuff and not the speakers! You change in your mind their truth and get a different story. That is how miscommunication happens!

Chapter Six- Assumptions of Life

In this chapter you will learn:

1. The natural way that we speak.
2. How easily and naturally we fill in the gaps.
3. How to start to listen to what is actually being said.
4. To understanding what is missing and what has changed.
5. What the best questions to ask are, in order to retrieve missing information.

In this chapter you will be able to answer the following questions:

1. What is our natural way of speaking?
2. Why do people misunderstand each other?
3. How can I get clear and concise information?

... I know what this is ... it is a tree! There are lots of trees here! What is this exercise all about anyway? I am told, I have to go and sit and notice what is in front of me. I see a tree, and next to it is another tree! And there behind it, yet another tree. There are lots and lots of trees. I am told that there are 73 different types of trees planted in this ground. They are all beautiful trees. I don't get it! What's the lesson here? What can I learn by just sitting here with my thoughts and looking at a whole lot of trees? Just trees ... big trees, small trees, very green trees, some red ones, some small ones. They are all different, even though we label them all the same ... we don't really but we do. We call them trees, although some are oak trees and some are maple trees. Some are fir trees, and some are pine trees. There are many trees, all the same and yet all different...

What have I learnt so far?

So far you have learned that we live in two worlds and we experience our world through our five senses. Once we have had an external experience, we store it in our neurology through those five senses. When we remember those experiences again, we remember them through our five senses. To better understand our thoughts we looked at the sub sections of our five senses, as this revealed our process for that particular behaviour.

By changing parts of the process, we are able to change the way we create that thought, which in turn changes the way we feel about that thought and ultimately the connection we have to that subject. We can reprogram ourselves to feel differently by becoming consciously aware and making changes to our life long programmes.

We have also learned that all our thoughts get translated into the body through the chemicals that we produce and this creates behaviour. To simplify, we call those chemicals brain juice and we subcategorised them into good and bad. We are able to tell what type of brain juice we are making by noticing how we feel physically. And by noticing how we feel, we can question whether it is appropriate to feel this way and make changes if necessary.

We have also learned that through our experiences we make "maps" which guide us to behave in a certain way. In other words, how do we know how to make a sandwich? In terms of maps, we would need a guiding system that shows exactly where to start, what path to

follow so that we finish at our desired destination. If our maps showed us putting mustard on ham before getting bread out etc., our sandwich would be a bit of a mess. The way that we respond to outside events is determined by what maps, programmes or scripts that we have installed in our neurology.

Without a guiding reference, we would not know where to start and where to finish. By the way, that is also why some of us feel overwhelmed at new tasks. We don't have all the internal information we need to execute the task and we become overwhelmed. Our maps are incomplete! This signal should be a trigger for us to go and find whatever information is missing, so that we can complete our tasks and not to become frozen with fear or have feelings of inadequacy.

There is a flaw in our internal system … If we live an unconscious life we have a natural tendency to reduce reality to simple words. This is done so that we can become more efficient in our everyday lives. However when we are not aware of how much we reduce, we start to impoverish the actual reality and take away flexibility from our internal world. It is as if we have hypnotized ourselves into a false reality that feels very real to us and so we operate as if this is true.

We start to believe that the limitations and obstacles are real and stop living the life we are meant to live. We begin to struggle and forget how to flow, to be happy and to live peacefully.

We fool ourselves to thinking that as we label things we know what they are and so we stop thinking about them. This puts our brains, who love habits and routines, into a pattern of 'stop thinking' and unconditionally accepting. We feel as if we are clear and we know what is going on, yet we are not aware that we have limited our experience to just words. All things in the world are magical for the way they function is on some level unexplainable. We can scientifically make sense of some of the functionality, yet there is still the magic of how it all really works. When we removed the 'magic' of something by not experience it consciously, we make it into a mystery by putting a word to it. How often do we walk out of our houses and not notice a new flower? Even if you notice the flower, how often do you appreciate the magic of the plant to create that flower. If you can come out of the sleep state of the unconscious living and wake up to a world that has so much more, you start to realize that no word in any language can give any one thing the depth of what it really is.

There is no way that a few utterances can reveal true meaning of anything. Although our system of generalizing is effective so that we can process fast, it can also be a hindrance as it takes away information that we need to be able to function in an easier way. When you start to look and listen to what is in front of you consciously, the words start to give new meaning and you start to regain the full experience with all its richness. Our reality is our optical internal illusion of what we think something is. As we begin to recognize this, we start to build flexibility in our lives and flow easier.

The trick is to be able to identify when it is necessary to recover more than what is being said, or when it's ok to leave it as it is!

> *Relying on diagnostics to solve psychological problems is no more effective than saying that a leaking ceiling needs a bucket to catch the water.*

The bucket is the technique that, for as long as you use it, it will work. The problem is that the bucket is not a natural solution, so in time it will no longer be effective, either because we forget to empty it and it overflows, or simply we get tired of empting it and now we are drowning.

Labels are just labels and by no means give us an accurate understanding of any situation or even better any problems. One word cannot, under any circumstances, fully explain the depth and complexity of any problem, no matter how simple or how complex it may be. All problems/dysfunctions even when sharing the same label are unique to the person who owns them. Effective solutions come from unique and effective discovery of how each of us creates our problems. Labels only give us a general understanding of what is most likely going on and a place to start the discovery.

When we listening to someone speak, internally we have to make some assumptions. In order to work, every sentence has to have some facts. It is not possible when we speak, to give all the facts of any particular event that we are describing and, as we mentioned earlier on, we have a natural tendency to leave information out, therefore altering the reality and generalizing the information. We can now feel confident to say, that when we hear someone speak, we know that there is information missing, changed and generalized.

However, sometimes we assume too much and distort what is there. We make things up and change the meaning of the sentence to what we think is being said and what we think they mean.

We also know that any emphasis made, is made out of the speaker's world and that it is their opinion and not necessarily the truth. For most of the time, this style of communication does not cause a problem. What we naturally do is fill in the blanks from our own map of the world to overcome this. We give it our own meaning and so the story becomes 'an according to us' version. We have to assume certain things within the sentence are true for the sentence to be logical.

As this is all natural and unconsciously done by all of us, how is it possible to communicate effectively and clearly? How do we avoid being misunderstood?

Adopting a conscious awareness while listening will help you to hear the assumptions enabling you to use skilled questioning to retrieve any information that is needed, so that there is no guess work.

This is the big secret that most people don't know. In business there is myth that if you know about open and closed questions and you understand eye contact, you have then passed enhanced communication skills. Yet most people that I have met still don't understand the basics of communication that I have discussed and therefore don't understand what goes wrong. Not many people have woken up to the fact that communication is an internal process and every word will conjure up internal images. If you leave things out, people will naturally and automatically fill in the gaps. And that is why we miscommunicate.

> *The big problem is that in the moment we are not aware that we are being misunderstood.*

By being able to understand more than just words, we are then able to demystify behaviour and what used to be unconscious, begins to be obvious. Up until that moment we live with the belief that we don't have the power to change as it seems all too complex for the average person.

The knowledge of how we create behaviour and how we translate that it into words enables us to change our maps which in turn will change our behaviour. It is all in the language. All our thoughts, all our fears, all our limiting beliefs can be heard by ourselves as well as others, if they know how to interpret our inner world where we live. If we can change our internal view of the world at that level, it changes our neurological output and we respond differently. We change as if by magic. Because internally we see things differently, we feel different and so we behave differently.

This is where we start to realize that our thoughts and feelings are symbols of our territory and not the territory itself.

...The longer I sit here with my thoughts and look at the trees, the more different they become. Is this my lesson? To sit here and notice how easy it is to just take away from something by labelling it with one general word? With a label I take away its essence, its beauty and its magnificence. Is it the same with other things too? Is it the same with books? They all have covers, pages and words! So all books are the same, yet they are all different. Flowers, all have roots, stems, leaves, flowers ... colours! All the same, yet all different. People ... all the same, yet all different!

I cannot possibly capture my essence, my spirit, my 'who I am' by just saying I am a woman or a man. The label doesn't do me or anything any justice! The label is just the starting point of discovery!

Exercise for you:

1. Make some time for yourself where you will not be disturbed and have pen and paper ready.
2. Think of something that troubles you.
3. Ask yourself what is it about this that troubles me?
4. What does it mean?
5. What else could it mean? (Go from the ridiculous to the sublime, just let your unconscious mind flow with ideas and reasons)
6. Ask yourself if what you think is true and what evidence do you have to support that thought?
7. Could it be that you are wrong and you need to change the way that you think about this situation?

Guru: How do you feel today?

Student: I know that today is going to be challenging!

Guru: How specifically do you know that?

Student: There are thoughts that I have been having that make me feel like sorting them out will be challenging.

Guru: What is your thought specifically about that makes you feel that way?

Student: Inside my head, my thoughts feel like they are mess and I don't know where to start!

Guru: If I had thoughts that were a mess, would that mean that I would find it challenging?

Student: Well no, you don't find anything challenging!

Guru: (laugh) so the perception about things being challenging is your stuff then? Who taught you this?

Student: (laugh) ah, you are always catching me out! My mom, she stresses about all things, like her home for instance, she will stress till it is in order!

Guru: Do you want to continue to allow your thoughts to make you feel this way? Can you allow your thoughts to just be? Can you sort them out without the need to also feel that they are challenging?

Student: I would want some sort of certainty to do that!

Guru: How would it look if you felt and acted certain that you could tackle all your challenges easily?

Student: It would look good and feel good. It is the thought that has to change, yeah? Am I getting it?

Guru: Do your thoughts still feel challenging?

Student: No

Guru: Then you are getting it.

Chapter Seven - We Alter Our World

In this chapter you will learn:

1. Why we alter our world.
2. What is the danger about altering our world.
3. What is the good thing in altering our world.
4. How do we hear it.
5. How to retrieve accurate information.

In this chapter you will be able to answer the following questions:

1. What do I do when I hear someone altering the truth?
2. How do I know what questions to ask?
3. How can I remember all this?

I want some confidence. I feel like I need some. Only then will I be ok. If only I could just get some now. I am impatient for this. Confidence to me says success. It is the only thing that stands in my way. Everyone knows that successful people are very confident, and I am just not confident enough. I know this will make the difference for me so that when I approach people about my product, I will not feel so insecure! I know that this is the only way to get ahead in my life ... or is it?

What have I learnt so far?

So far you have learned that we live in two worlds and we experience our world through our five senses. Once we have had an external experience, we store it in our neurology through those five senses. When we remember those experiences again, we remember them through our five senses. To better understand our thoughts we looked at the sub sections of our five senses, as this revealed our process for that particular behaviour.

By changing parts of the process, we are able to change the way we create that thought, which in turn changes the way we feel about that thought and ultimately the connection we have to that subject. We can reprogram ourselves to feel differently by becoming consciously aware and making changes to our life long programmes.

We have also learned that all our thoughts get translated into the body through the chemicals that we produce and this creates behaviour. To simplify, we call those chemicals brain juice and we subcategorised them into good and bad. We are able to tell what type of brain juice we are making by noticing how we feel physically. And by noticing how we feel, we can question whether it is appropriate to feel this way and make changes if necessary.

We have also learned that through our experiences we make "maps" which guide us to behave in a certain way. In other words, how do we know how to make a sandwich? In terms of maps, we would need a guiding system that shows exactly where to start, what path to

follow so that we finish at our desired destination. If our maps showed us putting mustard on ham before getting bread out etc., our sandwich would be a bit of a mess. The way that we respond to outside events is determined by what maps, programmes or scripts that we have installed in our neurology.

Without a guiding reference, we would not know where to start and where to finish. By the way, that is also why some of us feel overwhelmed at new tasks. We don't have all the internal information we need to execute the task and we become overwhelmed. Our maps are incomplete! This signal should be a trigger for us to go and find whatever information is missing, so that we can complete our tasks and not to become frozen with fear or have feelings of inadequacy.

In part two, we start to understand that the process of behaviour that we have now learned to understand has a flaw in the system. The flaw is that we are taught unconsciously to label things and events, so that we don't have to relearn them from the beginning, every time a similar event occurs. For the most part, this system works well. However, it also fails us from time to time and it is through our conscious awareness that we begin to pick this up and correct it if necessary.

The easiest way to hear and understand the flaws is through listening to the way that you or others present issues in speech.

Like we have mentioned before, in order for us to share with others and for others to understand, everything that we experience, that we think, that we believe and everything that we feel must be translated into speech. So it is in the speech structure that we use, where we can hear the flaws. We can also correct them if it is necessary and appropriate.

We alter the world that we live in, that is a given. Sometimes that is ok. If, however, what we alter distorts reality too much, it will cause limitations. The biggest problem with the altering that we do, is that we are conditioned and taught to either ignore it or, if we do hear it, to politely let it go. The patterns that we can hear in speech that show that we have altered reality are based upon our values and beliefs. If someone does not challenge those values and beliefs, then it enforces them even more and they become stronger and stronger. As powerful as this information is, unless you have permission to challenge it is best to leave well alone. Remember you are working with people's core values and beliefs and they will hold them very dearly. Random challenging may result in you having no friends! However when you get that feeling of resistance, you know that a belief or values inside of you has been challenged. At this stage if it is useful to change, keep going!

If we do not become aware of our internal voice and challenge what we are saying to ourselves then we too are subject to its' distortions.

So let's understand how beliefs are made. In our environment we have experiences. Let's assume that a baby crawls past a fire place and for the first time it notices the hypnotic and tantalizing flames burning bright. With fascination, the baby reaches into the fire place to touch and discover that these beautiful flames hurt and cause pain. The baby gets burned. So in the environment the baby has had an experience. The baby will instinctively now develop a strategy to avoid future pain. It learns to crawl out of reach of the fire place and discovers that its strategy works, and yes success ... no pain again.

What we now have is that through the experience we develop a coping strategy. What we don't know at this stage is if this is the best way to do things, for we lack experience and our references are limited. However, this strategy for now works so we develop a belief that this is right! We carry this belief unconsciously inside of us. If we share a belief with others because we feel that it will be for their better good so the belief now has become a value. Values are beliefs that are more universal and the purpose is bigger than us.

These alterations that we make in our reality are alright if the specific belief is one that benefits us.

As you will find out further on in this chapter, these patterns are subtle and go by unnoticed by most people especially to the untrained ear.

As you start to become aware of them, you will start to hear them more and more. The trick is to hear first in someone else, as normally there isn't an emotional attachment from your behalf. That way you stay rational for the sake of learning and just observe it for what it is. Then you can start to hear it in yourself and if necessary to challenge it or not. One of the mistakes I see eager new students make is to think that all reality alterations need to be challenged. They will go with this new skill and terrorise all their friends and family on everything they say. It is best to simply hear and observe and only when asked for help, to then elegantly use the questioning skills to retrieve and expose the real truth.

Let's look at the different language patterns in more detail.

Mental Assumptions

Very often we speak with a tone of knowing of what the future holds or what someone else is thinking and/or feeling. That feeling of knowing comes from us unconsciously gathering information and making a logical conclusion internally. If we have a whole lot of factors together we conclude that they must mean 'x'! In reality what we are really doing is guessing. The scary part is that it feels like what we think we know is real, when in fact it goes on an internal faith system that we have that only feels real. As we take feelings seriously, we unconsciously conclude that our feelings are right. They have after all not been cross referenced or checked! These factors that we put together go from a series of events that have resulted in the creation of a strong belief.

Seeing that we now have this belief inside, we now look outside of ourselves for visual and auditory evidence that we will match with what we believe. We all have an internal wanting to be right! So we will alter evidence on the outside to match what we believe on the inside. If someone has a low opinion of themselves, they will look for evidence to support their belief about themselves. They will go so far as to alter and reinterpret other people's behaviour to match their internal thoughts. That is why it is part of the world that we alter. Very often people have already made up their minds about something before anything is said or done. Someone will decide while getting dressed in the morning how their day is going to turn out even before they have got to work! They will then unconsciously look for evidence that proves them right. When people lack flexibility because they were never challenged to think outside the box, they are stuck with one interpretation to any event. Their belief feels even stronger because they don't have any other options.

Remember that our beliefs are made up of other people's beliefs and paradigms. We have been guided to experience the world in certain way and to believe things in a certain paradigm. Our beliefs may or may not be right, so when we look at this process that we so naturally do, we need to ask ourselves if what we know is right and would that be what we would choose to believe if we had the choice?

Talking of choice, we all have the choice, however if we are not consciously aware of our thoughts and feelings, choice does not seem to be something that we own.

Example:

'No one enjoys rainy weather'

'I know this is going to be a difficult six months'

'I am sure that you are aware that our company is thinking of entering a partnership with company x'

'You know how I feel about these things!'

'In two years' time, we will be in trouble with our mortgage payments as I don't think that we will be able to keep up!'

'This is going to be such a wonderful holiday!'

'The people on this team are real team players'

'I am going to love university'

The above sentences hint of a knowing either how the future is going to unfold or what someone is feeling or thinking. What is missing is how that person has that knowing. How did they come to that conclusion? Are

121

they guessing? Did someone go around the world and made a survey on everyone's like and dislikes of the rainy weather? Can someone really have a future knowing of the next six months? Did a manager go around asking everyone about their awareness of what the company is about to do? Does the partner ask if there was a knowing to their feelings? Does anyone know what their lives are going to be like in two years? Can anyone know if they will or will not be able to keep up with their mortgage payments?

On a more positive note, even if someone does not know how their holiday is going to turn out or whether their do have a team that are supportive or that university is going to be a good experience, the thought is a positive one. Earlier on in the book we mentioned how thoughts create our behaviours so in the case of resourceful beliefs, we simply let them go by. No need to challenge anything there.

In such simple sentences we can now start to see how something so subtle goes by unnoticed and therefore alters the reality that is.

The only distortions that need to be challenged are the ones that are causing problems and limitations.

The biggest give away for this particular language pattern are words like: I know, I realize, you are aware...etc. Sometimes, although the words are missing, you can still hear that they are mind reading and guessing! As you begin to recognise that this is happening, how do you retrieve the correct information? Simple, ask for what is being assumed.

Let's look at the previous examples again, this time followed by what type of question you can ask to retrieve more information.

Question:

'No one enjoys rainy weather'

Answer:

How do you know that no one enjoys rainy weather?

Question:

'I know this is going to be a difficult six months'

Answer:

How do you know that it is going to be a difficult six months?

Statement:

'I am sure that everyone is aware that our company is thinking of entering a partnership with company x'

Answer:

How do you know that everyone is aware of the company's thinking?

Question:

'You know how I feel about these things!'

Answer:

How do you know that he/she knows how you are feeling?

Question:

'In two years time, we will be in trouble with our mortgage payment, as I don't think that we will be able to keep up!'

Answer:

How do you know that you will be in trouble with your mortgage in two years time?

Question:

'This is going to be such a wonderful holiday!'

Answer:

How do you know it is going to be a wonderful holiday?

Question:

'The people on this team are real team players'

Answer:

How do you know that the people on the team are team players?

Question:

'I am going to love university'

Answer:

How do you know that you are going to love university?

I am the cause of my effect

In life there are all sorts of things that happen to us. Some of those things cause us to feel some sort of emotion. Depending on the event we will feel either good feelings or bad feelings. Sometimes those feelings make us feel like we are victims to an external circumstance. A person may feel that they have no choice about the way they feel. It is because someone else made them feel a certain way. When that happens we feel powerless to do anything about it for it is not us causing the event. The only way to stop the effect is if the person controlling the external event stops and puts us out of our misery.

This particular situation again can be heard through language patterns that the person uses to describe the event.

Again this is belief-based. This time instead of altering what is on the outside to match the inside, we now see, feel or hear what is on the outside and allow it to have

125

an effect or a certain feeling on the inside. What feeling we attach is determined by years of conditioning. We are taught and we self-learn how to feel certain things about different events through the experiences in our lives. We blame the outside world for how we feel on the inside. The truth is no one can make us feel anything without our permission.

"No one can make you feel inferior without your consent"

Eleanor Roosevelt, This is My Story, 1937

Often this is a truth that people don't want to hear, accept or do anything about. People have to get rid of their emotional crutch which can be daunting and scary. For a life time of habitual blame passing, taking ownership can be a difficult and an unknown act.

Example:

'It is not my fault that I am depressed, you would be too if you had my life!'

'You make me feel angry!'

'This project motivates me to work harder'

'My bosses shouting scares me'

'The economic situation is making me feel down'

'Sunny weather makes me feel good'

The logical truth is that no one can get into your head and mess with your neurology and change the chemical output in your mind so that it makes you feel a certain way. You are the cause of your effect. It is the way that you are thinking about the events around you. We look at some events with joy and some with sadness. Where did you learn to do that?

Think of something that makes you feel uncomfortable. Now, go back to your first year of life! Did you know how to do that feeling? If not, go to your second, third and so on. When and where did you learn it? You may say to me "I don't know, I don't remember!" That is ok. For it is not important to know the origin rather than to recognise that this is not a natural state for you but rather a learned state. It is more useful for you to recognise that if you were not born with the ability to do something you must have had to have learned it somewhere in your life. If you have learned it, you can unlearn it too. Change can happen the minute you recognise that you are actually in control. Take your power back.

Claim your freedom by claiming your responsibility to your own mind and your own emotional state. You and only you, are responsible for how you feel. Even if you are justified in feeling a certain way, it is still you that feels that. It is you in your mind that creates the chemical that cause the negative feelings. Is anything worth that! Is anything in the world worth you feeling tense or tired because you are not breathing properly due to fear or anger.

> *Think of all the negative emotions from a physiological point of 'you' and you ask yourself "What is this emotion costing my body?" Is there any thought out there that is worth your happiness, wellbeing and peace?*

Until you can fully accept this, the power is where you have placed it and therefore you cannot shift from where you are. Take it back and choose something better for yourself. You will instantly feel more resourceful.

Let's look at how we can use the right questions to retrieve what is hidden in our deep memory:

Question:

'It is not my fault that I am depressed, you would be too if you had my life!'

Answer:

What is it about your life that depresses you?

Question:

'You make me feel angry!'

Answer:

What specifically do I do that makes you angry?

Question:

'This project motivates me to work harder'

Answer:

How does this project motivate you?

Question:

'My boss's shouting scares me'

Answer:

How specifically does your boss's shouting scare you?

Question:

'The economic situation is make me feel down'

Answer:

How does the economic situation make you feel down?

What we are looking to retrieve, when we realize that there is blame put out there, is how specifically, can the external situation make someone have those feelings. What is the controlling factor? Often there is not enough information shared from the deep memory to reveal that information and so questioning will bring it out. Very often once the deep memory is expanded, the reason to feel a certain way is either dissolved or it becomes obvious that this is personal belief and therefore the feelings felt are by choice.

> *When you own a situation, you have power and control to change it if you want. You are no longer powerless.*

Example:

"He irritates me!"

"What is it about him that irritates you?"

"The way he leaves his socks lying around"

"If you left your socks lying around would that irritate him?"

"No, he doesn't care about such things"

"Do you have a belief that socks should not be left around?"

"..Well ... yes"

"Is it possible that he doesn't share your belief as you and that this is not personal?"

"Yes, I can see that. I am irritating myself!"

If one is true, the other is also true

As we grow up we learn about the world around us through association to something we already know. So in the beginning we don't know anything external, all is by instinct. We begin to learn about ourselves first and slowly we make connections in our mind to previous learning and so we build on this and our learning becomes faster and faster. In the beginning, the environment stimulates our learning and our thinking until it becomes predictable. At this point, we stop learning as much and thinking even less about what is around us. You can watch babies absorbing the information in the environment with total amusement and fascination. However, as adults we can step out of the same front door; go to our car and not notice how red our roses are, how blue the sky is or how butterflies settle gently on a flower.

It is part of our learning process to link something new to something old. Linking is a normal process in life and yet again it is also one that can cause limitation and leave us unresourced. If we link the wrong things together we can develop feelings that stop us from having the life that we want. In this pattern, what we will typically hear is two sentences that are totally unrelated. Most of the time, you can test the pattern by separating the two sentences and notice if each sentence can function on their own. Through association of linking one to the other, if one sentence is true it will automatically make the other one true as well. Most times the link is false and gives false meaning to the other sentence.

The information again lacks depth and integrity and so the real meaning can be retrieved from the deep memory by skilled questioning. What you will also hear is the limitation that the speaker puts on the circumstance that he is speaking about. There is now an illusion of an inflexible world when in reality the world is neither flexible nor inflexible. The world *just is!* The flexibility of our thoughts, however, will determine how our world functions.

> *The more flexibility we have, the easier the world that we live in becomes. The more choices we create for ourselves, the more options we have in how to live our lives, therefore the easier life gets.*

Often you will hear the 'because' word which then makes it a dead give-away! Again, I want to stress that it is not always necessary to challenge the structure. At times it is enough to hear and leave it.

Also most of the two previous patterns (mental assumptions and there is a cause to my effect) when challenged will turn into a linking pattern.

Example:

'I can't move on with my life, I am looking after my parents'

'I can't go on holiday because I can't save from my salary'

'I am smart that is why I am successful'

In all of the above sentences you can see that there are two parts to the sentences. Each part can stand alone. One part will be true and we can verify it. So let's look at the way we can challenge this and see if the link is a true.

Statement:

'I can't move on with my life, I am looking after my parents'

Question:

If I was looking after my parents would that mean that I could not move on with my life?

Or

If you were not looking after your parents would you be able to move on with your life?

Statement:

'I can't go on holiday because I can't save from my salary'

Question:

If I could not save from my salary would that mean that I could not go on holiday?

Or

If you could save from your salary would that mean you would be able to go on holiday?

Statement:

'I am smart that is why I am successful'

Question:

If I was smart would that mean that I would be successful too?

Or

If you were not smart would that mean that you would not be successful?

Sometimes the link that we have is about two totally unrelated events that are linked as if they belong to each other, when actually the one has nothing to do with the other. These sentences are more subtle and not as noticeable ... till you are made aware of them!

For example:

'Money is happiness'

'Marriage is stressful'

And the challenge is exactly the same as the other sentences with the similar structure.

For example:

Statement:

'Money is happiness'

Question:

If you didn't have money would that mean that you could not be happy?

Or

Can you only be happy with money?

Statement:

'Marriage is stressful'

Question:

If you were not married would that mean that you would be relaxed?

Or

If I was married would that mean that I would be stressed?

You can see that in each sentence, one part of the sentence is true and the other might be. Because the one is true, the brain automatically assumes that the other must be true as well because of the link. This is not always the case so, by testing it with a simple question to find a counter example, you can hear if the response is about a belief that the speaker holds or not.

Once again, we can hear that these patterns originate from our belief system and therefore, if they go by unchallenged, they become more enforced. Be careful to not challenge the positive comments as you most definitely want to enforce those.

Changing verbs and making them nouns

Our brains are so smart. We are smart! In order to function we do things in our minds in a very specific way, which is always the same! So here is what happens: We have a way of processing words that are things or nouns and we have a different way of processing doing words or verbs. Let's test this out:

1. Think of a chair.
2. Now ask yourself how do you represent the chair?

135

3. Do you see it as a moving object or as a stationary object?

My guess is that it is a 2D object that is stationary. After all a chair is just a chair. Until you give it more descriptions, it will have no function. Try it with more nouns like: table, bed, carpet, toothbrush etc.

Now let's think about verbs:

1. Think of jumping.
2. Now ask yourself, how do you represent jumping?
3. Do you see it as a movement or as something stationary?

This time I am guessing that the way that you represented jumping came across as a movement. You may have had to fill in the gap as to what is being jumped, however, there was movement in the way you represented that image to yourself.

As our brain treat nouns and verbs differently, we naturally have a different way of processing the information that is presented by each of them. Our brain has been trained to do nothing with nouns except for just making static images of them in our mind's eye and with verbs the brain puts movement to them. Now, in the English language, we have nouns that are real and then we have nouns that are not. What do I mean by this? Well think of it this way. If you can touch a noun and put it in a wheelbarrow then it is 'real'! If you cannot put in the wheelbarrow then it is not!

Here are some examples:

Chair – can go in a wheelbarrow

Table - can go in a wheelbarrow

Confidence - cannot go in a wheelbarrow

Apple - can go in a wheelbarrow

Communication - cannot go in a wheelbarrow

What does this mean? Let's look at these words in a sentence first.

1. I have a chair.
2. I have a relationship
3. I want confidence.
4. I want an apple.
5. I need sugar.
6. I need better communication.

They all present themselves as nouns. In the sentence 1, 4 and 5, you can clearly imagine what they would look like and you most certainly can put them all in the wheelbarrow. However, in sentence 2, 3 and 6, the image is hard to make as it is subjective and depends on what meaning you can attach to it. You cannot put them in a wheelbarrow. They are not tangible. Our brains do not know what to do with the information given by the noun until we have a verb that tells us what to do. So when we use nouns that don't fit in a wheelbarrow, the brain goes into a 'no solutions and do nothing mode'. It completely distorts the meaning of the words. Not a very helpful situation if you need better communication. By the way, 'situation' also can't be put into a wheelbarrow! So does any situation actually exist? I have a situation on my hands? Do I?

So what is the problem? Well we ask for things that our brain cannot process into an action to help create what we want. These words are also known as frozen words as they can't do anything. So when we use them, it is a no wonder that we feel stuck and frustrated with no idea how to move on.

What has happened in our evolution of verbal expression, is that we have taken verbs and changed them into nouns. This very simple process causes the 'stuckness' and frustration in our lives. The way to undo this, is to change the noun back into a verb or an adverb. By converting the noun back as verbs, it forces the brain to treat them differently, as we naturally have a different way of processing the information that is presented by verbs and nouns.

So once again, by questioning and changing the noun into a verb, it changes our internal picture and, as a result, changes the way we feel about it. We no longer feel stuck or frustrated.

Let's look at the examples again:

1. I have a relationship

    And how would you like to relate?

2. I want confidence

   How would it look if you were behaving in a confident manner?
3. I need better communication
   How would you like to communicate in a way which would make it better?

Here is a few more of those 'type' of nouns and how they look as verbs:

Communicate	Communicating
Love	Loving
Understand	Understanding
Conclusion	Concluded
Study	studied

Another way to check that there are nouns that should be verbs or adverbs is to put the word 'on-going' in the sentence. If the sentence makes sense then it not a real noun.

1. I have a chair.
   ... an on-going chair
2. I have a relationship
   ... an on-going relationship
3. I want confidence.
   ... on-going confidence

4. I want an apple.
   ... on-going apple
5. I need sugar.
   ... on-going sugar
6. I need better communication.

   ... on-going communication

Who said

Through our families and our environment we build beliefs and values. Most of the time we can't tangibly prove a belief that we have. If, however, our faith is strong enough we believe.

So what we will hear is a statement or an opinion that we have that is based on a value or a belief and we use as a fact. The evidence or the owner of the statement is lost so it is all based on pure faith from the speaker. We are working with unverified information. If questioned, it is very difficult to go back and identify who said it and where the statement originated from. In companies you often get the "we have always done it this way!" but no one knows why or even if it is still relevant to do it that way.

Here are some examples:

It is wrong to talk behind someone's back!

You must eat ice cream in the summer.

Smart people read books.

It is wrong to slow the group down.

The way to challenge this one is to question the 'who said' and if the sentence is still relevant it will be heard.

Let's look at those examples again!

It is wrong to talk behind someone's back!

Wrong according to whom?

You must eat ice cream in the summer.

Who said?

Smart people read books.

According to whom? Who said that smart people read books?

It is wrong to slow the group down.

Wrong according to whom?

It makes sense to me that I should be confident to get ahead so how can this thought of mine be wrong? Without confidence, I cannot do the things that I need to do. No ... I am right; to be successful I need to be confident. I want more confidence. When I have that I can be more successful. For when I have confidence, I will feel different and therefore I will be focusing on different thoughts. ...What if I changed my thoughts, will that change the way I feel. Could I just think myself successful? Would that thought make me feel more confident? Is this what they mean, that change happens on the inside before you see it on the outside? I think I was wrong in believing that I first had to be confident to become successful. In fact I know it! When I stop believing that I don't have what I need and start believing that I can be successful, then I will start to behave in a way that will give me what I want.

Change starts on the inside!

Exercise for you:

1. Go back to each of the different language patterns and one by one write some example of your own. They may be examples that you make up or sentences that you have heard people use.

2. Take your examples and write down how you would challenge them.

3. Also take one pattern at a time and watch unscripted interviews on TV and consciously listen for the pattern that you learning that day.

4. Make it a game, to listen to say 10 of those sentences per day!

5. You can also see if you can find them in emails or letters that you have written or received.

Guru: You are making great progress!

Student: It feels that way, though there are still things that worry me.

Guru: What things specifically?

Student: I want to start my business, but every time I think about it I get scared and my mind freezes and I don't move on. I feel overwhelmed and stuck.

Guru: Are there times when you think about starting the business and your mind does not freeze?

Student: Well... yes, I guess it is not every time.

Guru: When specifically do you freeze up?

Student: Every time that I think of getting customers.

Guru: What is it about customers that makes you freeze up?

Student: I keep worrying whether I will be able to get enough to support my business.

Guru: Do you know what you have to do, in order to get customers? Do you have the skills?

Student: Yes, I have done it for other companies for years! I am good at bringing business in.

Guru: I want you to imagine doing what you do best, and doing it for your company. How does that look?

Student: I initially feel uptight, but the longer I imagine it, the more it starts to flow and the more ideas I am getting.

Guru: So it is not every time, I wonder if it will ever be anytime again. Perhaps now it will be never!

Student: Yes, never, I will keep with the thoughts, relax and let the ideas flow. I don't feel stuck now.

Chapter Eight - Generalizations

In this chapter you will learn:

1. Why we generalize.
2. What is the danger in generalizing.
3. What is the good thing about generalizing.
4. How do we hear it.
5. How to retrieve accurate information.

In this chapter you will be able to answer the following questions:

1. What do I do when I hear someone generalizing the truth?
2. How do I know what questions to ask?
3. What does it mean when someone is generalizing?

I feel so overwhelmed ... it makes me feel like the whole world is on top of me. It is difficult for me to see a solution. Everything is important and all of it has to be done urgently. No one else can do this but me. I don't know where to start; all I know is that I must get the work done. This always happens to me. Every time that I have something important to do, every one brings me more work. I need to do it as soon as I can ... but I can't start. I don't know where to begin, there is so much work! I need to prioritise but I just don't how to start! I want to do the work well. I could do it step by step. I should have an order. I must get it right, and keep it up. I ought to if I want to keep my job! Take a deep breath!

What have I learnt so far?

So far you have learned that we live in two worlds and we experience our world through our five senses. Once we have had an external experience, we store it in our neurology through those five senses. When we remember those experiences again, we remember them through our five senses. To better understand our thoughts we looked at the sub sections of our five senses, as this revealed our process for that particular behaviour.

By changing parts of the process, we are able to change the way we create that thought, which in turn changes the way we feel about that thought and ultimately the connection we have to that subject. We can reprogram ourselves to feel differently by becoming consciously aware and making changes to our life long programmes.

We have also learned that all our thoughts get translated into the body through the chemicals that we produce and this creates behaviour. To simplify, we call those chemicals brain juice and we subcategorised them into good and bad. We are able to tell what type of brain juice we are making by noticing how we feel physically. And by noticing how we feel, we can question whether it is appropriate to feel this way and make changes if necessary.

We have also learned that through our experiences we make "maps" which guide us to behave in a certain way. In other words, how do we know how to make a sandwich? In terms of maps, we would need a guiding system that shows exactly where to start, what path to

follow so that we finish at our desired destination. If our maps showed us putting mustard on ham before getting bread out etc., our sandwich would be a bit of a mess. The way that we respond to outside events is determined by what maps, programmes or scripts that we have installed in our neurology.

Without a guiding reference, we would not know where to start and where to finish. By the way, that is also why some of us feel overwhelmed at new tasks. We don't have all the internal information we need to execute the task and we become overwhelmed. Our maps are incomplete! This signal should be a trigger for us to go and find whatever information is missing, so that we can complete our tasks and not to become frozen with fear or have feelings of inadequacy.

In part two, we start to understand that the process of behaviour that we have now learned to understand has a flaw in the system. The flaw is that we are taught unconsciously to label things and events, so that we don't have to relearn them from the beginning, every time a similar event occurs. For the most part, this system works well. However, it also fails us from time to time and it is through our conscious awareness that we begin to pick this up and correct it if necessary.

The easiest way to hear and understand the flaws is through listening to the way that you or others present issues in speech.

Like we have mentioned before, in order for us to share with others and for others to understand, everything that we experience, that we think, that we believe and everything that we feel must be translated into speech. So it is in the speech structure that we use, where we can hear the flaws. We can also correct them if it is necessary and appropriate.

We alter the world that we live in, that is a given. And to make the alterations easier we also generalize the things that we have learned. Now, generalizations are something we do very instinctively.

Once we learn to do something it becomes an unconscious act. Thus it feels like an instinct, as we don't pay too much attention to what we are doing.

If we did not have this process, we would have to learn everything over and over again every time we would want do to something.

So let's go back in time, right now. Imagine that you are 6 months old or so. There is something that you have not noticed before...something that later on you find out is a door. It is kind of there all the time. And it has something in the middle to the one side...later on you will discover it to be a door handle. So there you are sitting merrily on a pillow or a mat and you notice that your family... (You have figured that one out by now) move in and out of rooms using this thing that you have noticed.

As time passes you eventually figure out that this is a door with a handle and if you use the handle you can open the door and walk through it. You would be very conscious doing this the very first time in your life. That would be the first experience, and which-ever way it works out, you will achieve a result. As you keep having the same experience, you now have a strategy for moving in and out of rooms. Seeing that your strategy works, it now becomes a belief. By now you realize that this is just an event that you will uniquely label as 'opening the door'.

Now if you did not generalise this experience into a strategy you would have to learn what a door is and what a handle is and what you have to do with them every time that you come across them. In life you don't go to a house or office and be confused when you see a different door. You don't stand back in confusion wondering to yourself "how do I get out of this room?" So to make life easy we generalize … all of the time.

We do this with everything, so that we don't have to re-learn things in our everyday lives. It helps us function in an ever changing world that we live in.

However at times we tend to over generalize events in our lives with little evidence of the truth. On a map you will see signs to show churches, however you cannot see on most maps what church it is. We see signs for schools yet we can't tell if it is a high school or a primary school. When we over generalize, we once again impoverish our map of the world and give ourselves fewer resources to work with. We lose the detail that we need from the original experience. It is almost like we have taken a shortcut to make our life easier but instead we have under resourced it. What seemed to be a good idea for us to learn more and more has now backfired on us. Everything becomes the same and it is difficult to differentiate between tasks. The result leaves us feeling overwhelmed and stressed. The feeling of overwhelm and stress that we experience are as a direct result of a lack of flexibility and choice as to 'what else' this can mean and what other choices we have. For the unaware person, anyone that challenges them on their generalizations, would make them feel as if they are violating their reality which stems from their belief and causing them to become defensive for that which feels true; their belief about that particular situation.

In my experience when I hear people over generalize while explaining their situations, I know that they are stuck and they are not able to clearly see what solutions are available to them.

The best thing that you can do to help them is to coach them by helping them prioritise their tasks by order of urgency and importance.

Generalizations are not always a bad thing. Sometimes the lack of information helps us go forward and experience things that normally we wouldn't. When we generalize we make all similar things the same when in reality they are not. That would result in us getting resources from one experience that is unrelated to the experience where we need to feel resourceful. For example walking into a room will create a feeling in one experience, that is positive, and you could use this feeling *every time* you walk into any room, and be able to easily feel that positive feeling again!

The reason we learn to listen to how generalizations sound is to be able to identify them when they cause limitations. By skilful questioning once again you are able to elegantly reveal what is missing and bring detail and richness to the experience. The truth is now more obvious and so resources become available once again.

One world, one verdict

I had a client that wanted me to coach them on starting a business. I gladly accepted. She wanted to start a coaching school in South Africa. She went on to tell me that she was too scared to start a business because she truly believed that *everyone* would think that she was crazy to start a coaching school. That she was entertaining yet another crazy idea.

I asked who *everyone* was. For everyone implies the whole planet. Does it not? She looked at me as I was the mad one. Through our talk I narrowed it down, from the whole planet to just three people that she didn't care much about and had not spoken to in years!

It took me a whole five minutes, if that, to make her realize that her unconscious 'over generalization' stopped her from moving forward, for it took away her resources and limited her options. Her over-generalization scared her to the point of not being able to move forward! She felt frozen and overwhelmed in her fear. After I showed her and talked her through what she was doing, she was able to let go. She was able to feel the difference.

She looked at me and said *"that is stupid, is it not?"* Till that moment she had not stopped to ask herself if her fear was supported, real or helpful. She felt her fear and stopped moving forward with her dream. When I helped her see what she was doing in her mind, she was able to reason and laugh and simply stop scaring herself. Change does not have to be complicated or long drawn out. It also does not mean that it has to be super-fast either.

How would you know if you or anyone is generalizing? What would you hear? How would it sound like? Ever hear the words "Every time, everything, nothing, everywhere, nowhere, each, always, all, never, ever, no one, everyone" in a sentence? This usually indicates a generalization?

> *When we evaluate a statement with the equal measures to other things, what we are actually doing is taking away the individuality that it needs to help enrich the statement. The world now is a simple place that lacks detail. All trees are green, all skies are blue and all mountains are high!*

When you hear someone generalize you will hear certainty and assertiveness in their voice, even if it is the first time that they saying something. It comes from a deep memory that has certainty about the topic. Deep inside the unconscious mind has linked things together, so they will feel very certain that they are right. Because of the way that we link in the deep memory there is an unspoken expectation of how things should be, and when on the outside world things are different there is a feeling of disappointment. To the listener the sentence feels like an exaggeration that has not been well thought out.

Example:

- "*Everyone* will think that driving two hours to work is crazy."

- "I *never* get this right!"

- "This *always* happens to me."

154

What has to happen to stop this from limiting the speaker is find one counter example that will break the 'spell'! The minute you do this, the generalization is no longer there and so flexibility is back.

For example:

Statement:

"Everyone will think that driving two hours to work is crazy."

Question:

Who specifically will think that you are crazy to drive two hours to work?

Statement:

"I never get this right!"

Question:

Has there not been at least one time that you did get it right?

Statement:

"This is always happens to me."

Question:

Has there not been a time when this has not happened to you?

Sometimes the words that indicate generalizing are more subtle. Nouns which lack particular reference to one will automatically refer to many. A noun has to be specific or it loses important detail and information.

Example:

- *Men* must provide for their families.

- *People* go out on sunny days.

Again we look for to break the generalization and bring more detail to the sentence and with that, remove the limitation.

For example:

Statement:

Men must provide for their families.

Question:

Which men should provide for their families specifically?

Statement:

People go out on sunny days.

Question:

Which people specifically go out on sunny days?

By teasing the answer out, the person is forced to give more detail and it enriches the map which will then take away the generalization.

Moody operators

Most sentences will have words that regulate the mood of the sentence by converting the feeling of the main doing word or verb. They control the mood of the sentence. These words reflect a person's belief and according to where and which one they use, will reflect what they believe about different tasks. The interesting thing is that by simply switching one of these words it will automatically switch the mood of that sentence. Just one word has such power. The power, remember comes from a belief that they have in their deep memory which comes from previous experiences. You will be able to hear necessity, contingency, possibility, impossibility or qualifiers that people have about different tasks.

How they feel about their ability now becomes loud and clear, if you know how to listen. So I call these words mood controllers.

The moods that they conjure up are an array of different moods that we naturally experience. They can be from feelings of motivation to feelings of lethargy; feelings of confidence to feelings of obligation. The feelings that they create are the feelings that we have given them when we first started to use them. The power that they possess is the power that we have given them. The moods that each one of these words creates are unique to each and every one of us. It is

157

unique to the individual, so you will have to do some experimenting to find out what moods your words create for you!

It is important to find out what moods are created by different words for you. If you are using in your internal dialogue words that create apathy when you need motivation, it will cause frustration and a negative self-perception. You will find it hard to push yourself to achieve some things. For the same token you can find the words that motivate you to take action and use them on those tasks that you find tedious and just notice if you internally feel different towards the idea of doing the task.

What is very interesting is that it does not matter what the verb is, the way you feel about the task is determined by the mood controller. That is why this speech pattern falls under the generalization patterns. The mood controller will generalize the same mood to any verb!

Let's look at some of these words:

Possibility/impossibility	Necessity: (no choice)
Can/can't	Have to
Want	Must/ Mustn't
Wish	Should/shouldn't
May	Ought
Able	got to
Could/couldn't	Need
Get to	

might

Would/wouldn't

Will

And here they are in sentences. Notice what mood each one generates for you. You might want to take a note of each one. Try also some of your own verbs and notice how you feel with the different mood controllers. Notice if you feel positive or negative. Also start to notice what others around you use to motivate themselves, and when you have a task for them to do, use their word and simply notice how soon they get started. It can be fun and interesting to notice the power that these simple little words hold!

I am able to go to the gym.

I can go to the gym.

I want to go to the gym.

I could go to the gym.

I wish to go to the gym.

I may go to the gym.

I get to go to the gym.

I have to go to the gym.

I must go to the gym.

I mustn't go to the gym.

I should go to the gym.

I shouldn't go to the gym.

I ought to go to the gym.

I can't go to the gym.

I might go to the gym.

I would go to the gym.

I wouldn't go to the gym.

I really need to go to the gym.

I just want to go to the gym.

I jolly well ought to go to the gym.

Now you should have a good idea of what motivates and what pulls you away! Think of something that you thought you couldn't do or even something you really don't enjoy doing. Now replace the mood controller with the other mood controllers and notice if you feel differently about that particular task. It all comes down to observing yourself and becoming aware of which words makes the tasks at hand easier and which makes them harder.

For example:

"I must work", could possibly conjure up a feeling of lethargy. By changing it to say "I want to work", or "I have to work" or "I need to work", notice what mood you have now.

Experiment with the behaviours that don't inspire you and try on the mood controllers of the behaviours that do inspire you and notice the difference.

The other interesting thing that I have observed is that people will use a similar sequence of mood controllers for different events. So when you want to build rapport, or motivate someone to do something, it is best to use the same sequence when giving them instructions to what they should be doing.

For example:

Comment:

I *want* to finish the report, but first I *need* to get the resource files that we worked on and then I *must* prioritise the information. I *ought* to have this all done before the weekend.

Response:

Ok, that sounds good. I *want* you to let me know when you are done as I *need* to let the shareholders know when to schedule the next meeting. I *must* give them 1 weeks' notice, and then they *ought* to have enough time to clear their diaries to attend.

You may be thinking that people would notice that you are using their words in their sequence!! No, most people are so unconscious in what they are doing, that it will pass them by. However on the unconscious level they will feel a kinship with you for they will notice the similar patterns of speech that you are using.

In negotiations people will also use certain mood controllers in an order of priority. If they use the word 'need' that is not negotiable, the words 'want' has more flexibility and can be replaced by 'likes'. On the hierarchy of things, wants are more important than likes. If you know to hear this, you can negotiate likes for wants.

Take a look at this next example and notice the negations.

Estate agent:

So what do you need in a house?

Buyer:

I need 3 bedrooms, 2 reception rooms, a garage and a garden.

Estate agent:

What else do you want?

Buyer:

I want if possible an en-suite, a kitchen diner, a patio and that it is close to the schools.

Estate agent:

Is there anything else that you would like?

Buyer:

If possible, a cloak room downstairs, a conservatory a 3rd reception room and second garage.

Estate agent:

I have the perfect house for you! It has 3 bedrooms, master with en-suit, 2 reception rooms, a cloak room downstairs with a conservatory, a large garden with a big single garage and space to park a second car outside. It is close to the schools and in a quiet area.

As you can see the '*needs*' have been met and whatever '*wants*' could not be met, they were replaced with '*likes*'!

Changing the tense of the mood controller also creates an internal shift, so what was a limitation is no longer applicable. Subtle but really good to use!

For example:

Comment:

I have a real fear for spiders!

Challenge:

So when you were afraid of spiders had you noticed how you had responded?

Also what is important is when talking with children in a directive way that you remove all the mood controllers where possible and use sentences that I would term as 'clean talking'. Children are still developing and so it is easier for them to process commands and respond in a way that you want them if the command is 'clean'.

For example:

Parent:

I want you to put your coat on!

Child:

I want to play outside!

Parent:

I need you to put your coat on!

Child:

I need to go outside!

Parent:

You have to put your coat on!

Child:

No! I have to go outside!!

Parent:

You must put your coat on!

Child:

No! I must go outside!

Parent:

Put your coat on

Child:

…(reluctant) OK.

Step back and see what is going ... isn't that what I am supposed to do? Ok! I have to get logical. I have to get real. Are my thoughts true? They feel true! But are they true? I don't know. Is all of this work important? Do I need to do it all by myself? Do I have to do it myself? Can I delegate it to others and share the load? Is all that I am doing necessary? Am I making more work for myself? What do I have to do first? If I write all my tasks down, then I can start to prioritise one by one! Maybe it will start to get clearer and I will be able to see what work I can give to others. I will also be able to see what work is for me only! Just that thought alone makes me feel less stressed. I need to remember this so next time I can easily do this again ... this time with no stress!

Exercise for you:

Write different sentences out with both language patterns and notice how they feel and sound when you change:

1. The "one world, one verdict" word e.g. everyone to a counter example 'who specifically'.
2. The mood operator to any other and keep changing it till you have a good idea what stimulates you and what demotivates you.

Example:

1. No one wanted to play with me.

Mary, Anne and Jane don't want to play with me

Or

2. I need to finish my evaluations.

I must finish my evaluations or I can finish my evaluations or I should finish my evaluations.

In both examples, after you have made the change, ask yourself if that feels the same, better or worse? Keep making changes till you feel a lot better.

Guru: We lose so much of our world within our own thoughts.

Student: What do you mean by lose?

Guru: When we take things for granted, we live from a place of assumption. We think we know what we have seen, when actually we haven't. Our brains are clever enough to fill in the gaps, so that our internal experience still feels right. But it isn't for it is what we think it is.

Student: So what is the problem with that? If our brains do that, then it must be ok!

Guru: Sometimes it is, sometimes it creates a map inside of us that has lack. It is impoverished and unresourceful.

Student: How would I know the difference?

Guru: When you feel like you are out of options!

Student: That sounds easy … almost too easy!

Guru: It is, however without a conscious awareness of your thoughts and feelings, you don't notice this lack. Most people live unconsciously and are unaware.

Student: What does that effect, where would I feel the lack?

Guru: Mainly in your environment. Once you can recover the lost information, you are better equipped to make your unresourceful situation resourceful again.

Student: So when I feel a lack, the first thing to ask myself is, what is missing from my environment.

Guru: You are learning fast!

Chapter Nine - We Omit So Much From Our World

In this chapter you will learn:

1. Why we omit things out of our experience.
2. What are the dangers if you omit things.
3. What can you gain by omitting.
4. How do we hear it.
5. How to retrieve accurate information.

In this chapter you will be able to answer the following questions:

1. What does it meant when someone is omitting?
2. How do I help them retrieve information?
3. Where is this useful in business?

I am so tired of thinking; I just can't remember all the things that I need to do. There was a whole list. I just can't remember it. I should have written it down, but I really thought that I could remember it all. Now I wish I just did the old fashioned way and made a list. I just thought that others would think me stupid for not being able to remember it all. Maybe if I just start doing some work, then it will come to me. If I just do some tasks then maybe some of them will be what I was supposed to have done. At the very least, they won't think that I did nothing. I have been busy and I am hoping that what I do will have been part of the list that I should have done. Oh this anxiety is killing me. What if I spend a whole day working and I do nothing of what I am supposed to do? What if this gets me into trouble? I don't know what I'm supposed to do, this is terrible. I wish I had done the list. I suppose I could go back and ask, but then they will know that I don't deserve my job and it will be obvious that this is above me. I am really stupid. I am so stupid for not remembering the things my boss asked me to remember; stupid for not doing a list. I guess the only way to stop all this is to face up to what I have done...

What have I learnt so far?

So far you have learned that we live in two worlds and we experience our world through our five senses. Once we have had an external experience, we store it in our neurology through those five senses. When we remember those experiences again, we remember them through our five senses. To better understand our thoughts we looked at the sub sections of our five senses, as this revealed our process for that particular behaviour.

By changing parts of the process, we are able to change the way we create that thought, which in turn changes the way we feel about that thought and ultimately the connection we have to that subject. We can reprogram ourselves to feel differently by becoming consciously aware and making changes to our life long programmes.

We have also learned that all our thoughts get translated into the body through the chemicals that we produce and this creates behaviour. To simplify, we call those chemicals brain juice and we subcategorised them into good and bad. We are able to tell what type of brain juice we are making by noticing how we feel physically. And by noticing how we feel, we can question whether it is appropriate to feel this way and make changes if necessary

We have also learned that through our experiences we make "maps" which guide us to behave in a certain way. In other words, how do we know how to make a sandwich? In terms of maps, we would need a guiding system that shows exactly where to start, what path to

171

follow so that we finish at our desired destination. If our maps showed us putting mustard on ham before getting bread out etc., our sandwich would be a bit of a mess. The way that we respond to outside events is determined by what maps, programmes or scripts that we have installed in our neurology.

Without a guiding reference, we would not know where to start and where to finish. By the way, that is also why some of us feel overwhelmed at new tasks. We don't have all the internal information we need to execute the task and we become overwhelmed. Our maps are incomplete! This signal should be a trigger for us to go and find whatever information is missing, so that we can complete our tasks and not to become frozen with fear or have feelings of inadequacy.

In part two, we start to understand that the process of behaviour that we have now learned to understand has a flaw in the system. The flaw is that we are taught unconsciously to label things and events, so that we don't have to relearn them from the beginning, every time a similar event occurs. For the most part, this system works well. However, it also fails us from time to time and it is through our conscious awareness that we begin to pick this up and correct it if necessary.

The easiest way to hear and understand the flaws is through listening to the way that you or others present issues in speech.

Like we have mentioned before, in order for us to share with others and for others to understand, everything that we experience, that we think, that we believe and everything that we feel must be translated into speech. So it is in the speech structure that we use, where we can hear the flaws. We can also correct them if it is necessary and appropriate.

We alter the world that we live in, that is a given. And to make the alterations easier we also generalize the things that we have learned. If we did not have this process, we would have to learn everything over and over again every time we would want do something.

As we alter and generalize the world that we live in, we also leave things out. We omit facts. Now consciously we are not aware of this. However if it becomes a problem, then knowing about this little thing that we do, can help us fix what is not working. Our mind has been trained by us to focus on what we think is important, so in much the same way, we will not notice things or events that we think are unimportant. We simply ignore them. While in truth our conscious mind has ignored unimportant things, our good old unconscious mind has taken a lot more information in. Not all, but a huge amount more. So in the same way as with altering and generalizing, there in the deep memory we will have more information that we can use should we need it. When we leave things out, our map of the world lacks detail and full expression. It may lack information that we need. On the up side, leaving things out helps us from having too much information and making us feel overwhelmed and overloaded. So leaving things out is not always a bad thing and it also not always a good thing.

Once again if we have developed our personal awareness, we will notice what we are feeling. If the feeling is one of bad brain juice, then clearly it should be a signal for us to think about what is missing which is causing us to feel so unresourceful.

So often when one has such feelings, we are taught to panic, feel bad and freeze into the land of no solutions. What most of us haven't been taught is to take a step back, analyse the situation and ask ourselves intelligent and resourceful questions that will help us to shift into a place of resourcefulness and answers. What most people don't realize is that our brains are compelled to answer any questions we ask of it.

It doesn't matter if they are resourceful and clever questions or stupid questions, our unconscious will fulfil its duty and find any answer, right or wrong and deliver! Seeing that, when we are stuck, we ask questions like "Why is this happening to me?" or "Why am I feeling so bad?" it comes to no surprise that our brain will give us answers like "...Because you don't prepare, or you don't have confidence, or because you are not smart and never have been!" It will give out any answer. So, get into the habit of asking resourceful questions to retrieve the solutions that lie deep within you, that will create the shift that you want.

When you hear others, or yourself use statements that are incomplete, if appropriate, you can recover information with a simple list of questions. There are four ways that we omit information and depending on where the problem lies, will depend on what question you need to ask.

In my experience of working in the business environment, all too often you devise a list of question to ask your client, but seldom is one taught to understand what the answer gives. When we hear statements that lack clarity and resourcefulness what are brains are taught to automatically do, is to fill in the gaps. The problem with that is that what we fill the gaps from our base of knowledge and experience. It is our stuff, and not the speakers stuff. So, the minute we do this, we walk away with our version of someone else's story and not their truth. When someone gives instructions and the person who receives them goes through this process, the instructions change in an instant. I am sure it now starts to become more obvious how quickly miscommunication can happen. The scary part is, if you are not paying attention to your thoughts and feelings, this process goes by unnoticed. However, what you will notice later on is the mess it makes!

All sentences will have more than one thing that needs to be retrieved and sorted out. Not all are necessary and what makes a skilled communicator, is to know which one is going to create the biggest shift. That comes with experience, as you become more and more experienced with identifying all the different structures.

Basic omissions

Short and sweet sentences, that don't offer much information. There is much missing here and therefore, before you can go on you need to retrieve the rest of the sentence. As there is so much missing, it is difficult to understand the meaning of the sentence. If we ask ourselves what has to be true for this sentence to function, we soon find what is missing. The good thing is that most people trained or not, will naturally ask more to have a better understanding of what is going on.

For example:

I got it!

I understand!

This is simple!

To retrieve we use very simple questioning that comes naturally to most, for example:

I got it!

You got what?

I understand!

What do you understand specifically?

This is simple!

What is simple?

Where is the comparison?

This is such a simple and yet such a powerful structure. In this pattern you will hear a comparison, but what has it been compared to, has been left out.

In business you will often hear a client say "you are too expensive!" and the seller will go off to see what they can change to make the price more competitive for their client. Most of my customers had not thought of asking their clients a simple question "in comparison to what?" A little warning: you have to be prepared and aware of your competitors when you ask this question, so that you can justify your answer.

You will easily identify this pattern by hearing words like too much, too little, more or less or the "er" and "est" and the end of words.

You will hear words like:-

More than, less than, worse than, fewer, slower, best, better, too much, not enough, lower, higher.

Example:

Statement	How to retrieve information
It is much colder this winter.	In comparison to what winters?
This is the hardest thing I have ever done.	Harder than what?

This is not enough.	In comparison to what?
This is the best chocolate cake I have ever eaten!!	In comparison to what other chocolate cakes?
This quote is too expensive!	Too expensive in comparison to what or whom?

Unknown Verb

As with all the other sentence structures from this section, this too is simple. Here we will hear that our verb in the sentence lacks information. We don't know what is going on with it. The action is unclear. To some degree most of our verbs will be unclear. In most cases, this is really not a problem, and again by noticing you will be able to make an informed decision as to if you need to retrieve more information.

What you want to be aware of is for the listener making up actions inside themselves so that they understand what you are saying. This happens to some degree, what you need to watch out for, is that it does not happen to the degree of changing your basic information.

Example:

Statement	How to retrieve information
He run to me.	How specifically did he run to you?
He run away.	How did he run?

He laughed at her.	How specifically did he laugh at her.
He misinformed him.	How specifically did he misinform him?
He sang to the audience.	How specifically did he sing?

Unknown noun or pronoun

This works in a similar way to the unclear verb, with the difference that the noun or the pronoun is unclear. We don't know who or what we are referring to. The information is about the lack of information of the experience of the noun. You will hear the vagueness in words like "they" or "them" or "it" etc. Again, if there are no problems being caused, there is no need to find out more information.

Example:

Statement	How to retrieve information
That does not need to be here.	What does not need to be here?
They won't talk to me.	Who, specifically, won't talk to you?
Bring the notes to me.	What notes specifically must I bring?
Cook the meat for dinner.	What meat should I cook?

If I just do a lot of something and it is the wrong something, then that might be worse. I know that the right thing is to go back and ask. In the future I will know that no matter how stupid I may seem to look, I will have my notepad and I will write my list down. Actually, I see all my bosses write things down. Maybe, it is not so stupid. Maybe it is the smart thing to do. It is smart to have a list and plan your day and your activities. Here I am, thinking that making lists makes you look stupid. What is stupid is trying to be clever. I have learned! So this is what the famous saying of "if you fail to plan, you plan to fail" means! With my tail between my legs, I will ask for my list again, and from here I will always plan so that I can succeed.

Exercise for you:

1. Write a sentence of each of the four different sentence structures.
2. Write ways that you can retrieve more information.

Part Three

Katerina knows more…
but still gets caught up in life ...
Life just gets in the way!

Introduction

Why are we born? What is the purpose of our lives? Are we born to struggle, feel bad about ourselves, to feel broken, hopeless, helpless and worthless? Are we born with the purpose that we start happy and then as we grow up day by day we feel worse about ourselves? Are we meant to struggle to "make it" until we get to an age where we give up on the idea of making it and just accept that this is life! Some people get it lucky and therefore have it easy and others don't!

The quest for personal awareness and therefore personal development is to free ourselves from the thoughts that we have that make us feel inadequate in some way. We have a yearning to feel happy, calm and peaceful. It matters not whether that yearning comes from a memory that is so deep within us, we can't consciously access. Or is it because we have seen others and from our perspective they seem happy, calm and peaceful and therefore we want what we think they have?

Why is it then, that when people do all the courses to understand themselves they are only getting half way there? In my professional experience, I have met and worked with so many people that either start self-understanding with me, or have done some courses and just can't make it work. I have heard comments like "I know this works; it just doesn't work on me!" Or "My situation is different and this can't be fixed with just a self-understanding!" They struggle to integrate the learning with their behaviour ... and therefore with their lives. Some are selective. Parts of their awareness works, and parts don't. They will integrate some of the learning in their work environment and they get some success and some relief from the daily mundane stresses. However, in other parts of their life they are still struggling and in secrecy to themselves, still feel less than ... and not good enough! I have heard people recite back to me definitions and meanings of personal behaviour and still feel miserable and unhappy inside. Academically they know it all, realistically they are in pain.

Where do we see the symptoms? Everywhere. A sad and unhappy mind reflects it in different aspects of its life. The obstacles to personal success will manifest themselves in the four main areas of our lives:

- Relationships
- Health
- Finance
- Personal Perception

All problems in those areas will spill into each other. If you feel that you don't have enough money you may feel worthless, or if your relationship with your children is not good, you may feel as if you are not a good enough parent. If your health is failing, that might stop you from working, so you again struggle as you can't support the life you want. If your self-worth is damaged, you may feel you are not good enough to take the promotion. You may as a result of your self-image struggle everyday with your performance and live in fear that you will one day be discovered and as a result, lose your job. If people could see you from

your point of view, they may not like you! So we pretend that we are ok, and struggle inside.

Whatever it may be, it all comes down to a meaning that we have given any situation.

All situations come down to the beliefs that we have about ourselves. That we are helpless, hopeless or worthless.

However, where do we get our meaning and definitions from? Where did those beliefs come from? Are they truly ours?

My question to myself was "what stops people living happily?" Why is the learning not bridging the gap between a happy flowing life and a sad struggling life? Why with all the good intentions, the courses attended, the books read etc., do people still feel they have a life that is filled with stress, worry, anxiety, limitation and bad feelings in general?

Why have they forgotten who they are and what is important in life? And when they do realize what is important, why is that not enough to make the internal shift that brings about happiness, calmness and self-acceptance.

This observation troubled me. It troubled me mainly as this was part of what I went through. With all the right intentions, all the understandings, all the training I received and also delivered, why did I not feel complete or enough inside? And is it possible that is why clients and students feel the same? What is missing out of this understanding of self? What still needs to be taught or understood to make the change that brings about a life worth living?

My conclusion was that there had to be more to personal development than just a simple understanding of how we do things. There had to be more than just making changes on the surface. Personal development worked if we kept consciously aware of all our thoughts feelings and behaviours. It worked if we monitored it and made conscious decisions to make changes. However, if we're tired, overwhelmed by work, stressed and therefore are not monitoring, we default back to old behaviours. Whatever we feel about ourselves in our core, we will default back to. Not all of it, but the parts that were important. It leaves people feeling fed up and frustrated. It also leaves people feeling that this personal development "stuff" doesn't really work. However, it does work, but not on its own. The missing link is learning self-acceptance and realizing that you are whole and enough.

I think as a species that is so unique because of our ability to think, rationalise and have a conscience, we have come a long way in a short time. However there is more to us and I sincerely hope that this next section will introduce you to what more is out there for you to experience.

This next section brings you to the start of something deeper that creates changes. This part of your awareness is a start of happiness, calmness and inner peace. It is the start of self-acceptance and self-love on a level that makes the difference. It is natural. When you watch children play, they are natural and instinctive. They are happy and even if they fight, when the fight is over, it is over. They don't judge, or feel as if they are less than.

So up till now I have explained in broad terms that we have thoughts and although we have many thoughts, we only pay attention to a few. We decide that they are for whatever reason important, so they become important. Those important thoughts translate themselves into chemicals that travel through our nerves to every cell and every organ, passing information on what to do and what to feel. Our "brain juice" is either good or bad. We can very definitely feel what we are thinking by the way we feel. Nothing is random, even if it feels like it is.

We also looked at how we create thoughts, and how we experience the world through our five senses. We noted that when we remember events from our past or our future, again, we do them through our five senses.

Our experience builds a reference in our mind so that we have meaning to every experience as well as a map to be able to redo the experience again. All our behaviours have a beginning and an end. No behaviour is an on-going event. We start, execute the behaviour and then we stop. So we have created maps in our mind so that we can do things in an order that will produce the results that we want.

I also discussed that all our thoughts, feeling, behaviour, hopes and dreams can only be translated out of our existence and shared with others through the use of language. The way we speak reveals our beliefs about any particular event. By understanding the patterns we can easily start to have a deeper understanding of how we or anyone else feels about any certain situation.

Now, it is time to understand more than the surface part of you. It is time to go beyond the cognitive and start to work the intuitive part of who you are. It is the time to start to make changes that will bring lasting results.

Welcome to the rest of your life!

Guru: Have you ever wondered how your body knows how to do the things it does?

Student: No, but what things are you referring to?

Guru: Like getting scared or feeling inadequate?

Student: Mm, no, no thought. I know that my thoughts create the brain juice that creates the feeling, but I have not thought further than that?

Guru: Would you want to learn how to change the way your thoughts make you feel?

Student: Yes, of course, who wouldn't!

Guru: Once you have a thought it triggers a reaction in your body and with it an outcome?

Student: So our thoughts are triggers?

Guru: Yes! When you make a thought it will trigger off a response from its internal bank of reference. The thing that you haven't realized is that it also triggers off your internal dialogue.

Student: The yakadi yak or blah blah of my mind!

Guru: Exactly, and it is always the same combination. The thought will trigger the same reaction with the same commentary. When you become aware of it, you can consciously choose to change one of the three elements to shift the behaviour. By changing one you force the others to change too, as they exist in unison.

Student: Would that shift be permanent?

Guru: That is up to you. The more conscious you become around the behaviours that you want to change; the more you will choose to do something different. It is this pattern that creates permanent change, and the time required to create permanent change is individual to every person.

Chapter Ten - How We Create Behaviour

In this chapter you will learn:

1. What makes up behaviour.
2. What is the first thing that happens.
3. How do you change the behaviour.
4. What important questions can I ask myself.

In this chapter you will be able to answer the following questions:

1. Do I need to change my behaviour?
2. What things can I do that are easy so I can change behaviour?
3. Can I do this myself or do I need a therapist?
4. Is there a deeper meaning about myself that reflects in my behaviour?

I keep doing the same thing over and over again. I am so tired of feeling this way. I wish I could just stop doing what I am doing. Everything that I have tried has not helped me to stop... I feel so frustrated. I wish I could learn something practical that would also work for me, rather than just going around in circles. I am just so tired of being a victim to the triggers that make me feel so helpless...I wish I could find a different way to do things. I used to think that if I could understand I could stop doing what I am doing. I spent so many years talking to my therapist and still I have issues. I understand it more now, but I still feel frustrated, because the triggers from life still work to make me feel this way...

What have I learnt so far?

So far you have learned that we live in two worlds and we experience our world through our five senses. Once we have had an external experience, we store it in our neurology through those five senses. When we remember those experiences again, we remember them through our five senses. To better understand our thoughts we looked at the sub sections of our five senses, as this revealed our process for that particular behaviour.

By changing parts of the process, we are able to change the way we create that thought, which in turn changes the way we feel about that thought and ultimately the connection we have to that subject. We can reprogram ourselves to feel differently by becoming consciously aware and making changes to our life long programmes.

We have also learned that all our thoughts get translated into the body through the chemicals that we produce and this creates behaviour. To simplify, we call those chemicals brain juice and we subcategorised them into good and bad. We are able to tell what type of brain juice we are making by noticing how we feel physically. And by noticing how we feel, we can question whether it is appropriate to feel this way and make changes if necessary.

We have also learned that through our experiences we make "maps" which guide us to behave in a certain way. In other words, how do we know how to make a sandwich? In terms of maps, we would need a guiding system that shows exactly where to start, what path to

follow so that we finish at our desired destination. If our maps showed us putting mustard on ham before getting bread out etc., our sandwich would be a bit of a mess. The way that we respond to outside events is determined by what maps, programmes or scripts that we have installed in our neurology.

Without a guiding reference, we would not know where to start and where to finish. By the way, that is also why some of us feel overwhelmed at new tasks. We don't have all the internal information we need to execute the task and we become overwhelmed. Our maps are incomplete! This signal should be a trigger for us to go and find whatever information is missing, so that we can complete our tasks and not to become frozen with fear or have feelings of inadequacy.

In part two, we start to understand that the process of behaviour that we have now learned to understand has a flaw in the system. The flaw is that we are taught unconsciously to label things and events, so that we don't have to relearn them from the beginning, every time a similar event occurs. For the most part, this system works well. However, it also fails us from time to time and it is through our conscious awareness that we begin to pick this up and correct it if necessary.

> The easiest way to hear and understand the flaws is through listening to the way that you or others present issues in speech.

Like we have mentioned before, in order for us to share with others and for others to understand, everything that we experience, that we think, that we believe and everything that we feel must be translated into speech. So it is in the speech structure that we use, where we can hear the flaws. We can also correct them if it is necessary and appropriate.

We alter the world that we live in, that is a given. And to make the alterations easier we also generalize the things that we have learned. If we did not have this process, we would have to learn everything over and over again every time we would want do something.

As we alter and generalize the world that we live in, we also leave things out. We omit facts. Now consciously we are not aware of this. However, if it becomes a problem, then knowing that we omit things, can help us fix what is not working. Our mind has been trained to focus on what we think is important, so we will not notice things or events that we think are unimportant. We simply ignore them. In truth our conscious mind has ignored them, while our good old unconscious mind has taken a lot more information in. Not all, but a huge amount more, and as with altering and generalizing, there in the deep memory where we will have more information that we can use, should we need it.

When we leave things out, our map of the world lacks detail and full expression. It may lack the information that we need. On the up side, leaving things out prevents us from having too much information, and making us feel overwhelmed and overloaded. So

leaving things out is not always a bad thing, it is also not always a good thing!

In part three we start to explore the reasons why, with all the information, people still feel stuck or limited in themselves and/or in their life situations. What is the missing link to making permanent changes which bring about a flow in life? Why does personal development with all the right intentions not seem to work?

Let's explore behaviour in greater depth. What is behaviour? Is it something that you are, or something that you do?

It's something that you do. A simple way to tell whether something is a behaviour or not is to ask yourself "was I born with the ability to do it or did I have to learn it?" If you were not born with it, then you have learned it. All behaviour is learned.

Let's consider a behaviour, like walking. Were you born with the knowledge of walking or did you have to learn how to walk? My educated guess is that you learned to walk through a lot of repetition and a lot of intimate meetings with the floor. Now, ask yourself "are you a walking or is walking something that you do"? Are you a walk or are you doing the behaviour of walking? The answer is you are in the behaviour of walking.

The blessings about this information are this: One, you are capable of mastering things in your life. If you are rubbish at giving presentations and hate the experience, you a still a master at being rubbish at giving presentations and hating the experience. The second thing is that you can learn to do something different, because you have proven that you have the ability to learn a behaviour and master it.

> *When we give our unconscious mind only one way to do something, it has no choice but to do it that one way. If you build options or other ways to do things, the unconscious mind in all its wisdom, will always pick the quickest, easiest and healthiest way there.*

So when you are doing something over and over and you are miserable, stop and ask yourself "do I have another option?" The answer in that moment could probably be "not yet", even though you would love one! However, the fact that this is no longer unconscious, gives you the opportunity to change the behaviour and do something different.

Ok, what about emotions, are you actually happy, or sad? Good question isn't it? You see, people often take an emotion and they start to identify themselves as being that emotion, rather than saying this is what I am doing. What you should be saying is "I am feeling happy" or "I am feeling sad" instead of "I am happy" or "I am sad".

> *Two of the most dangerous and yet also most inspiring words are:* ***I AM!***

They form part of our identity. You may think that you don't mean it that way! Remember that your unconscious mind does not judge, or ask questions. It accepts the commands that you give it. So when you tell yourself that you are sad your unconscious mind says "yep, I know how to do that!" It is no wonder that we are unaware of why we feel bad. We experience our internal dialogue conversations quickly and unconsciously. When we identify ourselves with that emotion or behaviour, getting rid of that emotion or behaviour would mean getting rid of a part of ourselves. Your unconscious mind is always into self-preservation, so it will do whatever it can to stop and sabotage all your good personal development intentions and efforts!

Think about this. Basically we are all born the same; we were all born naked, hungry, curious loving and happy. Babies have no idea what they look like. They have no self-awareness and so they don't know if they are good enough and so they don't care if their nappy makes their bums look big or if their hair is ok today. They are not worried if their pram is a better and more modern than that of other babies. Provided their basic needs of food, warmth, being loved and having a dry bum are met, they are fine, happy and joyful little human beings. In our most natural and innocent part of ourselves that is actually who we are!

As we grow up we lose our innocence and our naivety. Yet in our deepest memory we still remember how it felt to feel loved, happy and joyful. That is what we are chasing to become and feel again.

When you ask people what they want, no matter what it is, when you break it down, it is all the same. We want love, peace, happiness, joy and to matter in our world. To know that being on this planet has a purpose that we can fulfil.

When someone says I want a new fancy sports car, it is not the metal body on wheels that they are seeking; they are seeking the feeling that driving that car can give them. The action makes them feel good, happy, joyful and important. There may be an underlining belief that others may think that they are successful and that thought gives them a feeling of accomplishment, in return that gives them a feeling of being good enough! Being good enough makes them feel happy! This last example is one where people seek from the outside world what only be found in the inside world.

As we grow we have learned to behave in ways that make us feel good about ourselves, accomplished, as well as inadequate and not enough. We may feel that there is a lack in us or in the way that we do things. We have this need to conform, to be accepted by those around us, so that we can be loved. We fear rejection

201

and being alone. We really don't like the idea of others not liking us. We fear that if we say what we think it won't be accepted. Yet at the same time we see others doing what we fear and getting away with it. Often we think "if I did that, I would get fired!" or something like that.

Can you relearn something again? In other words, can you start to do something that you had stopped doing? Yes, but why would you? Most of us learn unresourceful behaviours unconsciously when we were young and not with much experience or resources to do something better. As an adult with more resources than ever before, why would you consciously choose to feel bad? What does it say about you if you have put an unresourceful meaning to a particular behaviour?

It says nothing other than you did the best you could with the information you had at the time. Is it resourceful now? Perhaps not; however it only means whatever you want it to mean! Do you need a therapist to change? This all depends on you. For some people the simple realization that they have created this and that they can create something else is enough to make a shift. For others they will feel comfortable working with a therapist to help them create that shift. Therapists are not magicians. They can't do the work for you. However, I think they are catalysts, because they know how to help you create the changes you seek. All methods are good, as the only thing that is important is that you stop doing what limits you from living the best life yet. Stop whatever limits you and what makes you feel bad, and start to do what inspires you and what makes you feel alive! The more you do what makes you feel good, the more you will continue to do that.

By understanding the process of behaviour you will start to build flexibility and choice. So it is not always about getting rid of things, but rather giving yourself more choices. It will be more useful and easier to accept, if you build flexibility, for every behaviour has a place where it is useful. The intention of all behaviours are for our highest good. As things change in our life, sometimes, what was good is no longer needed. If you started smoking because you wanted to be part of a group, the intention was to be accepted. Today you can find healthier ways to behave that will create acceptance. So by focusing on how to do things differently in order to create the same emotional effect, it becomes easier, rather than fighting with yourself to stop doing something.

Like I said earlier, your unconscious mind will always choose the most ecological viable option. The more options you have the better the choices. If your original option is not used for a period of time, the connections in your brain will be become weaker and you will not be able to access those options easily.

Now, let's look in detail at the process of how we create behaviour, because once you learn what behaviour is all about, you can then start to change those behaviours that are not working for you!

To make every behaviour happen you will do three things:

- You will have an **thought**
- Your body will create a **reaction in your body**
- You will start an **chat with yourself**

These three things work together, instantly every time you do something!

Your thought

The first thing that happens for behaviour to exist is that we experience a thought. Without the thought there is nothing. The body is governed by what the mind tells it to do.

As we experience so many thoughts a day, it is interesting to try and work out how we decide what thoughts are important and what thoughts we let go. Earlier I said that thoughts are like clouds ... they just pass us by, unless we decide if they are important. What is more useful is to just notice and observe what we have unconsciously made important for that is the thought that will have an impact on us. In chapter 3, I explained how our thoughts are made up of a combination of our senses and by playing around with the sub sections of our thoughts we can change the way they make us feel.

Using that information to make changes, the most important question to ask yourself is "what am I thinking?" By getting an attitude of curiosity and becoming the observer of your thoughts you can now question yourself as to "is what I am thinking true?" "what evidence do I have that this is true?"

Your body

The second that the thought has occurred, you have two things happen. One is the physical manifestation. This is most obvious one to see, as it is what your body is actually doing at that moment in time. There's a physical manifestation for every behaviour. If you are walking, your body is actually walking, if you were talking your mouth will be moving, your face is showing different expressions and so are your hands.

What about the physical manifestation of emotions?

When we are looking at the physical manifestation, it is not enough to say I am angry. What you want to understand is how you do anger. How do you know that it is anger you are experiencing? What does your body do in order to experience anger?

What would your body be doing if you were feeling sad? Your shoulders would probably be slouching, your eyes would be looking down, you might be tearful and you are probably not breathing properly. You see, there are a whole lot of things that have to happen in order for you to be able to be feeling sad.

Let's look at anxiety; do you know what anxiety feels like? Anxiety would probably include tight/clenched muscles, shallow breathing, sweaty palms and a slightly unsettled feeling in the tummy.

How about something brilliant, how about confidence? How does your body look when you are feeling confident? It's almost like there's a magical string that pulls your spine up, and you hold you head up and your shoulders are back. The energy that you walk with is strong and energetic. Your eyes are sparkling and bright.

Using this information to make changes the most important question to ask yourself is "What is my body doing?" "What can I change?" Even changing something as simple as breathing can create big shifts. Our breathing tells us a lot about how we feel. When we change our rate and depth of our breath, we are able to tell our brain that we are feeling something different, and in return we get new and different brain juice.

> *Relaxing and softening our muscles will take us from a tense state to one that is relaxing. Again by changing our physical manifestation, you are now prompting the brain to create chemical change.*

Most of the time the brain through thought will stimulate the body. Where by changing the body, we stimulate the brain to change the thought.

A chat with ourselves

The other thing that happens directly after the thought together with the physical manifestation is that we have a commentary from our internal dialogue. Do you have an internal dialogue? Does everybody talk to themselves?

Ok, imagine you are at one of my seminars and I have just announced that I am going to pick someone in the audience to come up and sing their most favourite song! I am guessing that you had one of two responses; 'I wonder what song I am going sing?' or 'I hope she doesn't pick me, if I sit low down in my chair and not look at her, maybe she will leave me alone'.

Now, that little conversation you may have had in your head is your internal dialogue. We all have it and it works all the time. The voice inside of our heads guides us as to what to do, where to go and whether what we said is ok or not. It is our conscious, our feedback on what we are doing.

> *However what most of us have done is given the internal dialogue a promotion!! We have made it "DIRECTOR OF SELF CRITICISM!"*

Without any training, we promote the internal dialogue to become judge of who we are and how we are doing and we listen to it. Most of the time the internal mind consists of simple ramblings. Remember what I told you earlier in the book, whatever you ask your mind it is compelled to answer! Your Director of Self Criticism does not want to be found out for being under qualified, so it will answer with certainty and confidence with any old rubbish. I have heard people's internal dialogues, and most of the time they are harsh, rude and very unkind. Have you ever stood in front of the mirror and noticed what you say to yourself, or when some adversity comes through the letterbox, do you hear that little voice nagging. How about when you are asked to do something that you are not so confident about? What is the voice saying then? Is it words of encouragement and support? Would you use the tone and words to your child or a friend? So why are we listening to it?

Using this information to make changes, the most important question to ask yourself is; What am I saying to myself? Is what the voice is saying true? Is the voice yours? Try changing the voice, or changing the position and notice if it feels different. Out of the three aspects of behaviour, the easiest one to spot is the physical manifestation. It is unrealistic to think that you can be in control of every thought and every feeling. However, when it is one that is making you feel bad, let that be a signal for you to pay attention and begin to notice. Get into a state of curiosity and simply observe the three elements of behaviour and ask yourself the three questions that in themselves will take you out of the trance that you are in. It is difficult to keep an unresourceful state going if you are now observing it consciously.

As I have said the easiest aspect to change is the physical part. So if someone is depressed for some reason and feeling really down, I encourage them, really strongly, to go outside and hold their head up and smile and just walk, because the body says "if I'm doing all this and walking this is not the physical manifestation that equals depression". This also makes it very difficult for the body to then also keep up the internal representation, of the movie that we play inside our heads. You have to work very hard to keep thinking about all the adversities, about all the problems, while you are smiling and holding your head up high and just walking fast. As far as the brain is concerned that is not the formula for anxiety or stress or depression.

In summary, when you are experiencing an unresourceful feeling step back and say "STOP!" "What am thinking, what am I feeling, what am I saying to myself?" Look at your behaviour and ask yourself "what I'm I doing right now?" "How do I do this?" Now that you understand what behaviour is, you can control and edit it to work for you. All you need to do is change one aspect of your behaviour and it all changes. Once you go and do something different with your body, your internal dialogue or any other aspect we have mentioned, the brain will automatically change the chemical solution as this is not the right cocktail!

Now this sounds like a lot of hard work and in the beginning it may be. You have to re-educate your mind. However, feeling bad is a lot harder and a lot unhealthier.

Start by noticing if something is not quite right, notice that uncomfortable feeling, and think about it! Ask yourself "is my attitude wrong?" You might only notice this 10% by tomorrow, but that is 10% more that you noticed it today. By next week don't be surprised if you actually noticed it about 15% of the time. What you are doing is creating new habits for your mind and body to do. Personal awareness is a great contributor to all this.

I wish the understanding would make the triggers not work, I wish there was something easy and practical to use that would snap me out. OK, so let me step back and get logical. Thoughts stimulate my body. So if I understand the thought will that make a change, or do I simply change the thought. Change the way the thought works? Let me try ... if I take my thought and move it further away it does not feel the same. How about if I change the way my body has responded to my thought? I have tension on my neck and shoulders. I am breathing shallow. If I soften the muscles in my neck and shoulders and take deep breaths I start to feel as if my thought is not that important. The additional thing I have noticed is that there is a voice inside my head. What if I change that? What if the voice is not by my left ear, but I place it in the centre in front of me? What if I make the voice sound like Donald Duck? That sounds hilarious! I could not possibly take that serious. Wait a minute .... that thought just does not feel the same. It has changed. I am in control, I have always been! I am the master of my thought and my emotions ... of me. I always believed that understanding would bring me peace, however I have now experienced that changing brings me shifts that results in peace! All is well, I can do this again.

Exercise that you can do:

Think of something that you do that you wish you did not do.

1. Ask yourself how do I do that?
2. What am I thinking?
3. What am I doing?
4. What am I saying to myself?

Guru: How do you know what something means?

Student: I feel it?

Guru: Have you ever stopped to ask yourself, what is it that you are feeling? What does this feeling mean?

Student: Well, no, it is just a feeling?

Guru: What does it mean if you get angry?

Student: That I am not happy! I am making bad brain juice!

Guru: Yes you are, but what does it mean? Your unconscious mind is communicating with you, what is it telling you?

Student: I have never thought about it this way. That my unconscious is sending me messages. What does it mean?

Guru: It means that you had an expectation for someone or something to behave in a certain way, and they didn't.

Student: Like if I ask someone to post a letter for me and they don't. I feel disappointed because they have let me down?

Guru: Yes, that is a good example! Or perhaps you are going to an event and you have an expectation of how it is going to be, then it just isn't what you thought. Or you saw a movie after reading the book and you felt let down because the movie was not as good as the book!

Student: Yes, all those things have happened to me.

Guru: Disappointment requires adequate planning. If you are in touch with yourself you will become aware of this straight away, and then you can manage your emotions and understand what they are telling you.

Chapter Eleven - How Emotions Cloud Our Judgement

In this chapter you will learn:

1. What an emotion is.
2. What do different emotions mean.
3. What does this knowledge give you.
4. What do the emotions mean on a deeper level.

In this chapter you will be able to answer the following questions:

1. Why do I experience some emotions more than others?
2. How do I resolve the feelings that I am having?
3. What I am supposed to do when I feel bad emotions?
4. Am I supposed to suppress my emotions?

I am feeling so anxious ... it is almost as if I can't breathe! My chest is tight and I feel such tension in my neck and shoulders! I can't sleep well at night and in the morning I wake up exhausted. I am not even aware of what is causing all this, or that I am doing this. I know I worry a lot, but didn't think that it would make me feel this bad. I just want it to stop. I want to feel at peace again, and I just don't know how. How do I stop all these thoughts that are scaring me so much? How do I stop thinking of the future? Things are so unstable in my work. Jobs are being put at risk. I may lose my job and then what? How do I bring up my children, how do I pay for the mortgage, how do I feed my babies? How do I fulfil my role as a parent? I can't let them down. I made a promise to provide and protect. If I lose my job, how do I do that? It will be devastating. Horrible! I can't bear to think of it. The more I try to ignore it the more I think about it. I am supposed to stop thinking, how do I stop thinking? Is that even possible? I am supposed to change my thoughts to something more resourceful...

What have I learnt so far?

So far you have learned that we live in two worlds and we experience our world through our five senses. Once we have had an external experience, we store it in our neurology through those five senses. When we remember those experiences again, we remember them through our five senses. To better understand our thoughts we looked at the sub sections of our five senses, as this revealed our process for that particular behaviour.

By changing parts of the process, we are able to change the way we create that thought, which in turn changes the way we feel about that thought and ultimately the connection we have to that subject. We can reprogram ourselves to feel differently by becoming consciously aware and making changes to our life long programmes.

We have also learned that all our thoughts get translated into the body through the chemicals that we produce and this creates behaviour. To simplify, we call those chemicals brain juice and we subcategorised them into good and bad. We are able to tell what type of brain juice we are making by noticing how we feel physically. And by noticing how we feel, we can question whether it is appropriate to feel this way and make changes if necessary.

We have also learned that through our experiences we make "maps" which guide us to behave in a certain way. In other words, how do we know how to make a sandwich? In terms of maps, we would need a guiding system that shows exactly where to start, what path to

follow so that we finish at our desired destination. If our maps showed us putting mustard on ham before getting bread out etc., our sandwich would be a bit of a mess. The way that we respond to outside events is determined by what maps, programmes or scripts that we have installed in our neurology.

Without a guiding reference, we would not know where to start and where to finish. By the way, that is also why some of us feel overwhelmed at new tasks. We don't have all the internal information we need to execute the task and we become overwhelmed. Our maps are incomplete! This signal should be a trigger for us to go and find whatever information is missing, so that we can complete our tasks and not to become frozen with fear or have feelings of inadequacy.

In part two, we start to understand that the process of behaviour that we have now learned to understand has a flaw in the system. The flaw is that we are taught unconsciously to label things and events, so that we don't have to relearn them from the beginning, every time a similar event occurs. For the most part, this system works well. However, it also fails us from time to time and it is through our conscious awareness that we begin to pick this up and correct it if necessary.

The easiest way to hear and understand the flaws is through listening to the way that you or others present issues in speech.

Like we have mentioned before, in order for us to share with others and for others to understand, everything that we experience, that we think, that we believe and everything that we feel must be translated into speech. So it is in the speech structure that we use, where we can hear the flaws. We can also correct them if it is necessary and appropriate.

We alter the world that we live in, that is a given. And to make the alterations easier we also generalize the things that we have learned. If we did not have this process, we would have to learn everything over and over again every time we would want do something.

As we alter and generalize the world that we live in, we also leave things out. We omit facts. Now consciously we are not aware of this. However, if it becomes a problem, then knowing that we omit things, can help us fix what is not working. Our mind has been trained to focus on what we think is important, so we will not notice things or events that we think are unimportant. We simply ignore them. In truth our conscious mind has ignored them, while our good old unconscious mind has taken a lot more information in. Not all, but a huge amount more, and as with altering and generalizing, there in the deep memory where we will have more information that we can use, should we need it.

When we leave things out, our map of the world lacks detail and full expression. It may lack the information that we need. On the up side, leaving things out prevents us from having too much information, and making us feel overwhelmed and overloaded. So

leaving things out is not always a bad thing, it is also not always a good thing!

In part three we start to explore the reasons why, with all the information, people still feel stuck or limited in themselves and/or in their life situations. What is the missing link to making permanent changes which bring about a flow in life? Why does personal development with all the right intentions not seem to work?

We now know that three things happen to create any behaviour. We have an internal representation, a physical manifestation and our internal dialogue. When we change one of the three it forces our brain to change our brain juice which helps us to change the behaviour.

Emotions

The word emotion was first recorded in 1570 and it means to "stir up" or "to move out". The word derives from the original word "motion", so emotion is motion that we experience inside of ourselves.

We generally experience our emotions in our torso to be specific. So when we feel fear we might get a tight tummy. When we feel paralysed to talk, our throats tighten. When we experience anxiety, our chest tightens and we breathe short swallow breaths. Let me first explain a little of why that happens. You see we have two brains! The one is the obvious one which is in our head, otherwise known as the Central Nervous System and second brain is our Gut brain, otherwise known as the Enteric Nervous System. The nervous system lies between the sheaths of tissue of the oesophagus... or simpler said our food pipe to the stomach, small intestine and colon. This wonderful and sophisticated Enteric Nervous System communicates with the Central Nervous System (CNS) and gets information from our thoughts. It can also work totally independently if need be. If we have experienced an injury whereby our vagus nerve (one of the cranial nerves) is severed then communication between the two brains will stop, however the enteric system will continue to work independently. It is full of neurons and neurotransmitters and is able to produce a huge amount of chemicals similar to the brain juice made by the CNS. So now you know why you have butterflies in your stomach and a gut feeling about things.

So when we have thoughts the brain juice will communicate to the rest of the body and so, the gut brain gets the message too. All our emotions are felt in our throat, chest, solar plexus or gut area. When you get feelings from being scared, they do not begin in your knee or small toe. You may get jelly legs or sweaty palms, but those are physical responses and not emotional ones. Your feelings will be in your torso area, and typically they will move either clockwise or anti-clockwise or spiral down or spiral up. Simply by stopping the direction and then just changing it to the opposite way and holding on to the new movement can create a change in the way you feel about a given situation.

Our motivation to do anything is because of the way it makes us feel. We want to lose weight because of how we will then feel about ourselves. We want to buy a new bigger car, because we like the way that that makes us feel. When we go to a party, we buy new clothes because we want to look good; because of the way we feel when we look good. Our friendships and relationships are with people that make us feel good about ourselves. We don't want to stay in a relationship if it makes us feel bad – even if it takes time to get out... we get out!

We don't do things so that we can feel bad. At least not consciously. Yet all the feelings that we create that make us feel bad are made by us. We are the cause of the effect that we have, for we have chosen how to feel about circumstances. Some of the events we are directly responsible for and some we are not. However we are always responsible for the way we feel about things. This is again why it is important to have a healthy conscious awareness, so that we can become aware when we are feeling bad. In other words it helps to quickly realize that we are making bad brain juice. When you leave yourself powerless to the outside world, you become a victim of its wrath. You have no control over what happens in the outside world. Yet you do have control over your emotions. Your emotions are all good. Even the emotions that create bad brain juice are good. What is not good is when you get stuck in them and do not hear the messages they are giving you.

Most of us are without realising it ruled by our emotions. In the following chapter I am going to explain to you just how you create these emotions, what they are actually telling you and how to use them as they are intended.

From time to time we all have gut feelings about situations. Good or bad, we feel things. We get feelings about people, ideas or future events. This happens because your unconscious mind is able to absorb a lot more information than your conscious mind. We are not aware of this process, however if we test it we can prove it. The conscious can only focus on 7 + or − 2 process at any given moment. In much simpler terms we are able to execute between 5 and 9 processes. The question of "how many processes?" will depend on the complexity of the process and our ability to do them. That ability comes from our experience. For example: A child learning to ride a bicycle cannot perform the act of balancing and pedalling and steering the bike. Most kids will focus on the one to the detriment of the other. I have seen my daughters not knowing to take their feet off their pedals and so when the bicycle stopped they fall over ... feet still on the pedals. However, I have seen a cyclist in Holland, riding a bicycle hands free, talking on the phone and turning a corner. Once we have gathered more capability through experience, then we are able to process more. This process is called learning! All this time the unconscious just takes information in, while still filtering bits out. The unconscious doesn't absorb everything... and thank goodness for that it would be information overload, but takes in a huge amount of information. So it would be fair for me to say that you know more than you think you do. This is also why we work on the assumption that when people want something, they have the resources to achieve what they want.

Sadly though, most people want what they unconsciously know they can have, yet they consciously stop themselves from getting it, because they feel as if they can't get it.

The simple excuse is that "Life gets in the way". When the unconscious mind wants to give you information it does it so through your emotions. Have you ever set out to do something or go somewhere, but have that niggling feeling that something is not quite right, maybe I shouldn't bother? But you say "nonsense ... rubbish" and you override that feeling and you go anyway. How often did those events turn out to be a disaster and you say "I knew it! I knew I shouldn't have gone there, I knew I shouldn't have left the house!" That was your unconscious giving you information that you chose to ignore. How many people have been taught to listen to their inner voice, their gut feeling, and their instincts? It is not fluffy weird stuff, it is your inner wisdom screaming at you so that you can give it some attention and act in a way that is useful for you.

I have chosen to write about the emotions that are the most common, negative emotions, as they are the ones that cause the problems. In my world, if it is not broken, step away from the picture. Leave it alone. Always.

Let's look at our emotions:

Fear:-

Fear is an emotion that can cripple people and cause inaction when it is just a warning to check that you have got all the information you need. It is your unconscious mind making sure that you know what's going on and that you have prepared well enough for a situation. So when you get scared, it is your unconscious mind trying to communicate with you and to make sure you are ready. Pilots have a physical check list that they use before every take-off and landing. Our checklist is from within us.

When you write exams, sometimes you get anxious or scared. It is your unconscious mind checking with you. All you need to do is consciously reassure yourself that you are ready. If you are not ready, accept where you are and do the best you can.

Going in to an exam with an unresourceful feeling is not going to help you find information you don't know, but it can stop you from getting information you do have, which is really not very useful. Being scared and not acknowledging your feeling before a presentation can actually help you forget all the things you want to remember. Again this is not a very useful behaviour. By checking with yourself, you may come up with things that can improve your presentation that otherwise you would have missed.

If you come home and for some strange reason you feel scared, it is probably your unconscious mind that is picking something up as different, and it is giving you a warning. It may not be anything serious; however you can be more consciously aware of your environment and check it out. When you feel fear, simply ask your unconscious "what is my brain trying to tell me, what is it warning me about?" You would be surprised how precise your inner voice can be.

The feeling of fear is also the opposite of confidence. Confidence is a feeling that so many people seek for all sorts of different reasons.

When we are not feeling confident what we are feeling is fear.

Often the fear will be about checking that you are prepared, but often the fear is about us humiliating ourselves. We are so scared that people will discover that we are not good enough, or perfect, or as capable as we think they want us to be. We are scared that if we fail in the eyes of others, they will see us for who we are and then will not like us any longer. On a very deep level, fear is an expression of worthlessness. We may not feel worthless in all aspects of our lives, but fear of being discovered is, there is also a belief of self-worth.

The truth is that if you want to become more confident you need to overcome your fear. So it is not confidence that you seek, for that does not exist, therefore your search will lead you to frustration and failure. You seek to learn how to be more courageous and brave and do the things you want to do!

> *We are able to be courageous and brave in other words "confident" if our self-worth is intact.*

If we feel deep inside, the feeling that even if I do rubbish, I am still ok, then we feel brave enough to try. To build confidence you need to be prepared to get it wrong and still approve of yourself and love and encourage yourself to keep going because you are worth it.

What you can do: Think of all the difficult times in your life and ask yourself how did you survive them? As I have said before we are built to survive and make it through any adversity. So whatever happens, we survive. No one died from giving a bad presentation speech or from a first date or wearing the wrong clothes. However our mind is so powerful and can imagine all sorts of things. Ask yourself "Is what I am fearing real?" or "What is the worst thing that can happen ... is that so bad?" Again our personal awareness can help us to realize that our thoughts are just like passing clouds in the sky. You can observe them with an attitude of curiosity and just watch them move on. We cannot control all of thoughts. We cannot control what thought we are going to have next, however we can control how we feel about the thought, and whether we want to give it meaning and importance. My advice to you is that life is not a dress rehearsal. Your time is valuable, so choose with care what is important and let the rest go... for they are all just thoughts... passing by.

Anger:-

Anger is a very interesting emotion because it is actually what I would call a secondary emotion as it masks something else. It stems from a belief of helplessness, as we don't have control of our external circumstances. We get angry as an expression of what we are feeling deep inside, which is something different. It could be a feeling of rejection, inadequacy, disrespect, or a feeling of being ignored. We build expectations of how people should treat us, however this is unconscious. It comes from our values and beliefs that we have been taught about how to treat people. We feel people should treat us in a certain way and when they don't, the anger comes from our helplessness in not being able to control them or the environment. When we have an expectation from someone or something that has failed us, we get angry. Imagine that you have an important letter to post. For one or another reason you didn't prioritise and did not manage to post it. You therefore ask someone else to do it. For them the letter means nothing. They don't know why it is important. They don't have your map inside their heads. So they don't post your letter. Your expectation has failed and you get angry!

228

You go on a holiday and there is a promise from the travel company about what the resort will be like. You now have an expectation of what your holiday is going to be like. However when you get there, it is nothing like you expected ... you get angry.

You have separated from your partner and you feel some emotional pain but accept the situation. You do though imagine that it will take you and your ex some time to get over this before you can start to date again! Next thing you hear that your ex-partner is dating already. Your expectation has been crushed and you get angry!

Sometimes you are the one that is letting yourself down ... you expect yourself to be more disciplined with say food, and then off you go and eat a slice of cake. You get angry at yourself for not having the willpower. Perhaps you want to write that book and you don't put the time in. You get angry at yourself for procrastinating.

Maybe you promised yourself that you won't go out on a date with your ex-partner, it is not healthy. Yet on the next phone call you get, you agree to see them and after the weekend together you are angry at yourself for being "weak".

So what is anger about? You get angry because you expect that something or someone is not behaving in a way that you expected. You expected a certain outcome that didn't happen. You expected a person to behave in a certain way and they haven't ... maybe they didn't get your memo. Maybe you don't have as much control over people and situations as you would like to have.

In broader terms, things just don't work out as you expected and as a result you get angry.

What can you do: The question now is "how do I stop getting angry?" When you get angry instead of going completely with the negative emotions inside and all the bad brain juice that goes with it, stop and ask yourself "what is this telling me?" "What expectation did I have?" or "Did I really truly have control over the situation, could I really expect this person to do this for me or should I have done it myself?" or "Did I know better? Am I angry at myself actually?" "Could I have been more proactive and done something different a week ago? Should I have spoken to someone a week ago and sorted this thing out, whereas now it's become a problem?" Being able to objectively look at your thoughts and what is creating the anger will open a door way to the route of the problem and also the solution you want.

Hurt/sadness:-

Sadness is that emotion that leaves us feeling physically heavy-hearted. Again, like anger there is an expectation that we had that has not been met. Unlike anger though, sadness comes from a deep feeling of hopelessness. There is a feeling of loss. Nothing can be done. It is hopeless, it can't be fixed and that causes us the pain and hurt that we feel. Sometimes we lose a dream of the future, sometimes the loss is about our expectation to be with someone from the past and now we have lost them.

The outcome of this emotion can be one of total inertia or lashing out and causing more pain.

> *Hurt people tend to hurt people.*

Step back when someone says or does something that is hurtful to others. What is their pain that drives that behaviour? If we feel good and peace full inside, we don't have a need to hurt others, or to prove to ourselves that others have painful lives like ourselves. The "we are all in the same boat" so to speak is not needed to make us feel better. We don't need to hurt other so that we don't feel so bad about our lives.

Sometimes the loss is one of trust either with others or with our self. In one way or another whatever you expected is lost and the situation feels hopeless and difficult to recover.

Truth...? We all have problems. No one lives the perfect life. We all have fears, problems, limitations and inadequacies. We may feel that ours are worse in comparison to others, but that is again in our mind. We build thoughts that tell us so. Not many people will openly share their negative traits and feelings about themselves. So we have a perception of how others feel about themselves and what their lives are like by the way they seem on the outside, and compare ourselves with them.

What can you do: The most resourceful thing to do is compare yourself to who you were yesterday? Have you grown, have you developed? Are you further down your path of life? What can you do differently? Ask yourself the intelligent questions "what I am feeling is according to whom"? Or "If I could, would I want things back?" "This loss that I am feeling, can I do anything about it?" or "do I need to allow myself time to grieve?"

Anxiety:-

Anxiety is an emotion of the future. We get anxious about what might happen. The deeper belief around anxiety is that we are helpless. It is common for people to worry about things that might happen. Research has shown that of all the things that we worry about only approximately 10% comes true. So it is very possible to have the most miserable life, in the comfort and safety of your own home. We imagine how things are going to be in the future and we feel helpless in those situations. However in the moment we naturally become very resourceful and survive. The problem, as have discussed earlier in the book is that the brain can't tell the difference between fantasy and reality.

> *So as you are imagining the worst in the comfort and safety of your home, your brain is producing negative stress chemicals that are causing you physical harm.*

If something in the future is so important, that you will now spend time worrying about that future event, then why when the event becomes to the present, do we ignore it and focus on a new future event? When is now the right time to change that? I would say now!

What you can do: Get real with that thought you are having. Ask yourself "Is what I am predicting real?" or "what certainty do I have about the thoughts that I am having?" Ask yourself "if that is to happen, is there anything I can do to prevent or change it?"

Stress:-

Stress is an emotion that puts pressure internally on us to perform in a certain way. It must be pointed out that there is healthy stress, otherwise known as eustress. This type of stress is considered helpful and fulfilling. However the stress that I am refereeing to is the one that causes unresourceful states, sleepless nights and arguments.

It is a chemical response that happens automatically when we feel that we are under threat. Because we are human and we are more sophisticated than any other life forms, we experience stress in three different areas of our life. We have physical stress from events like car accidents, falls, injuries or going from a wide range of different temperatures, not enough rest or bad diet. This could also be anything that actually takes the balance from your physical body and disrupts physical harmony.

Then you get emotional stress which includes all the worries about our future, our finances, our children, our health or loss of loved ones. This is anything that causes an imbalance in us, from the way that we feel about things.

Lastly we experience chemical stress which is induced in us from toxins in the air, chemical in foods, from fertilizers or pesticides, etc. Chemical stress creates physical stress in us which in turn creates an emotional stress. For the same token any bad emotional situation can in turn cause a physical stress. For example your worries over your career can cause you to have a stiff neck and shoulders, and a physical injury can cause chemical stress.

No matter what stress we experience the body will react in the same way. It changes our physiology by changing our blood pressure, our heart rate, our pupils dilate and we experience a chemical change in all our cells and all our organs. The body releases high amounts of adrenalin and glucocorticoids. These are chemicals that help the body take immediate action. The problem lies that we are not like other animals, whereby after the initial danger, we quickly return to normal and let go of what has just happened. When we hear bad news, or worry about something in the future we can hold on to those thoughts for weeks and months and so producing stress hormones in our body for long periods of time.

> *We learn how to do stress in our body, so with each new time, we can do stress easier and quicker.*

As the stress is mainly generated only from thought, this starts to result in chronic stress. More and more research is finding that long term illness is caused by stress related situations.

Stress comes from a deep belief of helplessness. There is a feeling that there is no option and no control. I must/have to/need to do it, seems to be the common feeling. Sometimes we don't want to do certain things, or we don't know how to do them. So we don't do them. But we must do them, so when there is enough pressure inside of us, we force ourselves to do those tasks. However now we are doing them with negative energy that we have accumulated and unresourceful states, creating chaos and disruptiveness inside of us. Are we doing this to create more drama in our lives, or are we too scared to say no and follow another path?

What you can do: Become aware of your thoughts. Even if it causes you to feel tension in your body. Most of your stress will come from thoughts that create chemical changes in your body and have an impact on your physiology. Your thoughts are powerful to say the least, and to not take this serious is to say, I know I am powerful but so what! Analyse your thoughts and question yourself as to: is what you are thinking so terrible? Can you do anything about the situation you are worrying about?

Summary table of our emotions to our beliefs

Emotion	Belief
Fear	Worthless
Anger	Helpless
Hurt/sadness	Hopeless
Anxiety	Helpless
Stress	Helpless

Emotions are just a way for your brain to communicate with you; they are absolutely brilliant if you use them in the right context!

Here are some tips on what you can do when you are feeling unresourceful:

1. The most important step to controlling your emotions is to be able to become aware of them. Realize when your body is feeling unresourceful feelings, and simply ask yourself "what am I feeling?"

2. Become logical and accept that your emotions are from you and they are not trying to sabotage you but rather help you. Focus inward and ask yourself "what message does my emotion have for me?"

3. Ask yourself "why am I feeling this way?" What is motivating this emotion?

4. For every emotion you have, there is for a reason behind it. Have a conversation with that emotion, by acknowledging it, accepting it, loving it, forgiving that part of you that creates this emotion. A conversation with your emotion could be something like this:

   - Thank you for being here.
   - Sorry I have tried to ignore you for so long ... I didn't know how to handle you.
   - I forgive you for the pain you have created, forgive me for ignoring you.
   - I accept that you are part of me and you belong to me.
   - I love you for you are a part of me and you make me complete.

5. Think of the times that you have had bad situations happen and gather evidence of your resolving and surviving all situations in the past.

How do I do that? I am so anxious that I just find it so difficult to change something that I feel is happening automatically to me. Let me think, what is my emotion about? I am feeling anxious... in other words fear of the future! I don't know what the future will bring. I am guessing... that makes more sense. I can't allow this to happen to me on just a guess! I have no evidence that this is true. I now remember... in the eye of the storm all is calm. I am of a species that fights for survival. I have the resources I need to do whatever I need to do to survive and overcome. I am more resilient than I recognise. In the adversity in my past, no matter how bad the situation, I was able to overcome. I need to give my brain better instructions, better questions, so that I am empowered rather than squashed! It is within me to change, to control my emotions, by questioning and controlling my thoughts. I have no proof that this is going to happen, and if it does I have no proof that I won't survive. I let go of those thoughts, for they do not serve me. I choose to trust in myself and in life. All is well in my world. Life is good!

Exercise for you:

Think of a situation that makes you feel uncomfortable.

1. Ask yourself what emotion am I feeling with this situation.
2. What is my unconscious mind telling me?
3. What is the message I have not been listening to?

Guru: Do you know what the secret to living easy is?

Student: You mean you know and have not shared this with anyone?

Guru: Oh I share it alright, only to those who are ready to listen.

Student: But surely everyone would want to listen. Who would not?

Guru: Those who are still fighting with their ego.

Student: So what is the secret to living easy?

Guru: Allowing yourself not to have the need to judge.

Student: I don't judge. I believe in the "who am I to judge."

Guru: Yes for others, how about judging yourself?

Student: What does that feel like? How would I know if I am judging?

Guru: Every time you have an opinion or a meaning for something you have judged!

Student: Well that would be for everything?

Guru: Yes, so the secret is to be able to notice, be curious and just let it go by without a need to know what it is or what it means.

Chapter Twelve - Staying Neutral

In this chapter you will learn:

1. What does it mean to stay neutral.
2. What are the benefits of this state.
3. When is it important to be neutral .

In this chapter you will be able to answer the following questions:

1. How do I stay neutral?
2. What will I notice in a neutral state?
3. How does it feel to be neutral?

I have thoughts all the time of how I want to feel. I just don't understand my emotions. I wish I could understand, nothing is making sense, and yet it doesn't feel so difficult. I feel that if I could understand I would be free of these feelings. Would I be free? I don't know anymore. I am supposed to work out my past and my connections, and then I will have a deeper understanding of myself... but the more I dig in my past the more upset I get by what I remember. I don't even know if what I remember is real or not. Am I making things up? What do I do? I just wish none of these feelings were here to haunt me. I wish I could feel differently. I wish I didn't feel this way...

What have I learnt so far?

So far you have learned that we live in two worlds and we experience our world through our five senses. Once we have had an external experience, we store it in our neurology through those five senses. When we remember those experiences again, we remember them through our five senses. To better understand our thoughts we looked at the sub sections of our five senses, as this revealed our process for that particular behaviour.

By changing parts of the process, we are able to change the way we create that thought, which in turn changes the way we feel about that thought and ultimately the connection we have to that subject. We can reprogram ourselves to feel differently by becoming consciously aware and making changes to our life long programmes.

We have also learned that all our thoughts get translated into the body through the chemicals that we produce and this creates behaviour. To simplify, we call those chemicals brain juice and we subcategorised them into good and bad. We are able to tell what type of brain juice we are making by noticing how we feel physically. And by noticing how we feel, we can question whether it is appropriate to feel this way and make changes if necessary.

We have also learned that through our experiences we make "maps" which guide us to behave in a certain way. In other words, how do we know how to make a sandwich? In terms of maps, we would need a guiding system that shows exactly where to start, what path to

243

follow so that we finish at our desired destination. If our maps showed us putting mustard on ham before getting bread out etc., our sandwich would be a bit of a mess. The way that we respond to outside events is determined by what maps, programmes or scripts that we have installed in our neurology.

Without a guiding reference, we would not know where to start and where to finish. By the way, that is also why some of us feel overwhelmed at new tasks. We don't have all the internal information we need to execute the task and we become overwhelmed. Our maps are incomplete! This signal should be a trigger for us to go and find whatever information is missing, so that we can complete our tasks and not to become frozen with fear or have feelings of inadequacy.

In part two, we start to understand that the process of behaviour that we have now learned to understand has a flaw in the system. The flaw is that we are taught unconsciously to label things and events, so that we don't have to relearn them from the beginning, every time a similar event occurs. For the most part, this system works well. However, it also fails us from time to time and it is through our conscious awareness that we begin to pick this up and correct it if necessary.

The easiest way to hear and understand the flaws is through listening to the way that you or others present issues in speech.

Like we have mentioned before, in order for us to share with others and for others to understand, everything that we experience, that we think, that we believe and everything that we feel must be translated into speech. So it is in the speech structure that we use, where we can hear the flaws. We can also correct them if it is necessary and appropriate.

We alter the world that we live in, that is a given. And to make the alterations easier we also generalize the things that we have learned. If we did not have this process, we would have to learn everything over and over again every time we would want do something.

As we alter and generalize the world that we live in, we also leave things out. We omit facts. Now consciously we are not aware of this. However, if it becomes a problem, then knowing that we omit things, can help us fix what is not working. Our mind has been trained to focus on what we think is important, so we will not notice things or events that we think are unimportant. We simply ignore them. In truth our conscious mind has ignored them, while our good old unconscious mind has taken a lot more information in. Not all, but a huge amount more, and as with altering and generalizing, there in the deep memory where we will have more information that we can use, should we need it.

When we leave things out, our map of the world lacks detail and full expression. It may lack the information that we need. On the up side, leaving things out prevents us from having too much information, and making us feel overwhelmed and overloaded. So

leaving things out is not always a bad thing, it is also not always a good thing!

In part three we start to explore the reasons why, with all the information, people still feel stuck or limited in themselves and/or in their life situations. What is the missing link to making permanent changes which bring about a flow in life? Why does personal development with all the right intentions not seem to work?

We now know that three things happen to create any behaviour. We have an internal representation, a physical manifestation and our internal dialogue. When we change one of the three it forces our brain to change our brain juice which helps us to change the behaviour. But it is not that simple! We have emotions that cloud our judgement and then it is difficult to make the changes. Now we learn emotional mastery. What do the emotions that cause problems mean and what can we do to change them.

All up till now we have dealt with the events of our behaviour once they have happened. The one thing that comes to mind is that what we are doing is a bit of chaos and damage control. For many cases that is ok. However the ultimate is to find a way that allows you to be in a state of self acceptance and harmony and not have to do all the stuff to change our states after the event so that you can be happy. In other words to be in a state of bliss! Most people will say that is impossible to be in 100% of the time. I agree. So what is the ultimate?

The ultimate is balance. Living a life that is about raising children, developing careers, getting what you want from the world, and having spiritual harmony.

So many schools, without knowing it, encourage the thought of becoming one with the world and losing your individuality. Others courses teach you how to notice your uniqueness and achieve your personal power. The ultimate for me is to notice that you are both and as you embrace the universe as a part of you; you realize your uniqueness and strive to live a good life.

In my opinion the problem about most personal development programmes, is that they take you from one restrictive life to another.

The first restrictive life is one that you have already created and want to change. You may not want to change it all, but there are elements that you want to change. You may be ok at home but at work there are things you wish you felt differently.

The second restrictive life is the personal development world. We jump on the self-help books and seminars, in hope to change, to improve and be rid of dysfunctional behaviours. If we do what we are told, if we follow the rules and keep ourselves consciously aware, we can keep the bad feelings at bay.

The fault in that, when we are bogged down with work, tired; overwhelmed we flip back to what the unconscious knows to do. So can change be permanent? Yes, but often it takes time. There is a promise that it is quick and instant and definitely permanent. Often though it does not happen that way.

What stops us? From all the things that I have read, the people I have worked with, as well as from my own experiences, what stops us is how we feel about ourselves. How deserving are we to change.

What we fail to realize is that we complicate things. We have been taught to do that. We have not been taught to keep things simple and easy. We are taught that life is hard, and change is difficult. Anything simple and easy just doesn't fit our belief criteria.

So if there is a way to do that, why all the information until now? The information is necessary, otherwise the leap is too great... In my experience people are happy to make a smaller leap than one large one. Learning happens when I bolt one piece of information on to something that you know. The unconscious mind accepts it as it is not strange or different. For you to learn you need to be able to trust the source and suspend all your beliefs so that you can open yourself to new ideas and new learning.

This is an age of awakening. We are more advanced than ever before and our technology in the world is developing faster and faster. We must be prepared to step up to the next level and for that we need to trust the new information and be prepared to let go of what was. You can't accept the idea that you are free and deserving to live the life you want, and still feel that you have to comply with rules because you are worthless of your own ideas. It just can't be. The thoughts are conflicting.

You can only let go of what was, if you understand what you were doing, else what are you changing?

Conscious awareness brings to the light how you feel and how you respond to situations.

It helps you question the importance and validity of situations. It brings the question of what can I do differently now? How do I get to stop what I am doing? Without the information that you have received until now, you wouldn't be at the point of knowledge of yourself.

Where you want to go from here is to a point of living and not managing. How do you achieve that?

Everything that you know in your life you have given it meaning. It all has to mean something. We are taught to understand things by what they mean. If we don't do this when we see something we don't know what it is, because it does not mean something.

When we don't have all the information, we fill in the gaps, for it is more important to give meaning, so that we can understand rather than to not understand.

In order to attach meaning we need to judge something. So judgement is what happens in our mind in an attempt to give meaning to things. Meaning defines us, for by judging we can understand and label ourselves, our environment, our behaviours.

What you see in the world and what you experience is a replica of what you think the world is... which stems from the way you judge the world. Absolute reason of anything does not exist for it only has the meaning that you have given it. The meaning of your life is what you have given it. No one shares your meaning. You choose what things mean, and so the life that you are trying to run from or change, is the one you are constantly creating.

There is no hidden agenda or divine intervention conspiring against you. It is just you and your thoughts.

To be in a state of nothingness, would mean that you can't judge. Judging comes from our ego state of knowing, how things should be and then making a comparison and deciding, this does not measure up! Someone (usually your parents) has already unconsciously decided what things in your life mean and they pass that information by the way they behave on to you from birth and as a result you unconsciously continue this judgement throughout your life. Till now you have been living a script that tells you how to feel and what to do.

True happiness comes from a thought of what your place in the world is and how you fit within your world.

When you learn to simply observe a thought, you can start to choose what you want that thought to mean. Imagine that you have a situation and you observe it. At this stage you have not given it any meaning ... so it is meaningless. Now you can decide what you want it to mean, if anything at all. Imagine that there is a buffet full of emotions, and you can, for a change, choose any emotion you want ... what would you now choose?

Think of the stories you have about yourself and why you can't do certain things. If you had no meaning, what meaning and emotion would you choose to give those events?

If you don't judge, things have no meaning, therefore they just are. When you do things in life, and sometimes you don't get the outcome you want, it is enough to just say I can improve but I am ok. No judgement of self is needed if we are ok with whom we are.

You are precious and perfect and no thought should take away your self-worth.

I have to breathe, and relax. Soften my muscles and simply relax. Now watch the clouds, and notice and observe my thoughts. Step back and just be in the moment and notice my thoughts. No meaning, no judgement. Just observe. It feels like I am watching a movie of myself ... but not get into the movie. Simply watch ... observe, keep breathing deep and relax. From here my thoughts are just thoughts. Some are interesting, some are really boring! I have such silly thoughts! Most of them are actually useless! I have never felt this way about my thoughts. I wish I was taught this at school. Now I can watch my thoughts and simply observe and let them go by ... just like clouds. No need to make any of them important.

Exercise for you:

Think of a situation that you would want to feel differently about.

1. Observe it in your mind.
2. Take out any emotion you have for that situation.
3. Let go of any meaning you have.
4. Ask yourself, if I was to choose a meaning, what meaning would I choose?
5. If I was to choose an emotion, what emotion would I choose?

Guru: We are at the end of this journey. How do you feel now?

Student: Calm, I like the lesson on having no meaning for things.

Guru: It puts you back in control of your life. Now you start to create a life that is your purpose, your choosing, your creation.

Student: For the first time I feel ok with everything around me. I know that not all is perfect … oops judgement ... but you know what I mean, and I am ok with that!

Guru: Perfection lies in the imperfect world. When we can acknowledge that, then we live with peace.

Student: And also I feel so brave to go out there and just do the things that I have been so scared to do! That is exciting.

Guru: For you now it is important that you not only live your life well, but teach this to others by doing. People learn by what they see, not what they are told.

Student: Yes your right! Thank you, you have given me back what has always been there for me. My life to live.

Guru: You have always had, but were too blind to see. All that you need is within you.

Student: For the first time, that makes sense. I had heard that saying so many times, and now I can say that I understand it.

Guru: That is growth!

How Does This All Fit Together in Real Life?

Conclusion –

How Does This All Fit Together in Real Life?

In this chapter you will learn:

1. What the bigger picture is.
2. Why is it important to live consciously.
3. Where did I learn to be this way.

In this chapter you will be able to answer the following questions:

1. How do I let go?
2. Do I have to change everything?
3. How do I remember all the things I have learned?

The ramblings of my mind have taken me on a journey that has been a learning adventure. I have learned about my thoughts, my feelings, and the process of my behaviour. I have learned about the way I say things, and what they mean, and why I am still stuck...

How Does This All Fit Together in Real Life?

What have I learnt so far?

So far you have learned that we live in two worlds and we experience our world through our five senses. Once we have had an external experience, we store it in our neurology through those five senses. When we remember those experiences again, we remember them through our five senses. To better understand our thoughts we looked at the sub sections of our five senses, as this revealed our process for that particular behaviour.

By changing parts of the process, we are able to change the way we create that thought, which in turn changes the way we feel about that thought and ultimately the connection we have to that subject. We can reprogram ourselves to feel differently by becoming consciously aware and making changes to our life long programmes.

We have also learned that all our thoughts get translated into the body through the chemicals that we produce and this creates behaviour. To simplify, we call those chemicals brain juice and we subcategorised them into good and bad. We are able to tell what type of brain juice we are making by noticing how we feel physically. And by noticing how we feel, we can question whether it is appropriate to feel this way and make changes if necessary.

We have also learned that through our experiences we make "maps" which guide us to behave in a certain way. In other words, how do we know how to make a sandwich? In terms of maps, we would need a guiding system that shows exactly where to start, what path to

follow so that we finish at our desired destination. If our maps showed us putting mustard on ham before getting bread out etc., our sandwich would be a bit of a mess. The way that we respond to outside events is determined by what maps, programmes or scripts that we have installed in our neurology.

Without a guiding reference, we would not know where to start and where to finish. By the way, that is also why some of us feel overwhelmed at new tasks. We don't have all the internal information we need to execute the task and we become overwhelmed. Our maps are incomplete! This signal should be a trigger for us to go and find whatever information is missing, so that we can complete our tasks and not to become frozen with fear or have feelings of inadequacy.

In part two, we start to understand that the process of behaviour that we have now learned to understand has a flaw in the system. The flaw is that we are taught unconsciously to label things and events, so that we don't have to relearn them from the beginning, every time a similar event occurs. For the most part, this system works well. However, it also fails us from time to time and it is through our conscious awareness that we begin to pick this up and correct it if necessary.

The easiest way to hear and understand the flaws is through listening to the way that you or others present issues in speech.

How Does This All Fit Together in Real Life?

Like we have mentioned before, in order for us to share with others and for others to understand, everything that we experience, that we think, that we believe and everything that we feel must be translated into speech. So it is in the speech structure that we use, where we can hear the flaws. We can also correct them if it is necessary and appropriate.

We alter the world that we live in, that is a given. And to make the alterations easier we also generalize the things that we have learned. If we did not have this process, we would have to learn everything over and over again every time we would want do something.

As we alter and generalize the world that we live in, we also leave things out. We omit facts. Now consciously we are not aware of this. However, if it becomes a problem, then knowing that we omit things, can help us fix what is not working. Our mind has been trained to focus on what we think is important, so we will not notice things or events that we think are unimportant. We simply ignore them. In truth our conscious mind has ignored them, while our good old unconscious mind has taken a lot more information in. Not all, but a huge amount more, and as with altering and generalizing, there in the deep memory where we will have more information that we can use, should we need it.

When we leave things out, our map of the world lacks detail and full expression. It may lack the information that we need. On the up side, leaving things out prevents us from having too much information, and making us feel overwhelmed and overloaded. So

leaving things out is not always a bad thing, it is also not always a good thing!

In part three we start to explore the reasons why, with all the information, people still feel stuck or limited in themselves and/or in their life situations. What is the missing link to making permanent changes which bring about a flow in life? Why does personal development with all the right intentions not seem to work?

We now know that three things happen to create any behaviour. We have an internal representation, a physical manifestation and our internal dialogue. When we change one of the three it forces our brain to change our brain juice which helps us to change the behaviour. But it is not that simple! We have emotions that cloud our judgement and then it is difficult to make the changes. Now we learn emotional mastery. What do the emotions that cause problems mean and what can we do to change them.

However, at the end of this we learn that when we move into a state of nothingness, we stop judging and start accepting. From this place we are able to decide what things mean and what we want to feel about them.

How Does This All Fit Together in Real Life?

Conscious Living

When we read a book, what makes the book interesting is the story held within the pages. What we are reading is someone's life story, and it doesn't matter if the story is true or not. What captivates us, are the events within the story. In the way that the author writes, we are able to visualise the main person, the places and the other people that are in the story. We can see their physical appearances and feel their character. We even build an opinion of them ... when most of the time they don't even exist ... except in our world of fantasy.

Whatever the author wants us to experience, within the words on the page, we can experience. Whatever the author wants us to focus on within the words of the page we will focus. Because that is how that story is written. All other facts that happen around the story are deleted so that only what is important is in focus. Our attention is controlled by the author's intent.

In much the same way, we all have a story of our lives. By our standards and our point of view, our story is real and meaningful. The things in our story really happened. And yet that story only gives a person a glimpse of their whole life. So much is left out. We too, like any author, will tell the parts of the story that we think are important.

We too will control the attention of the story depending on what we intend to emphasise. As we tell our story we too will only reveal what we think is relevant to whom we are. We too, delete so much of our story. We generalize so much and skip years to get to the next part that is important. We alter the feelings to be what we feel it is. All the editing of our story is according to our point of view.

Look into your photo album and see the evidence. Photos show a glimpse of our lives. They don't show us feeling inadequate. They don't show us feeling sad or scared. However I want you to just contemplate for a little while. From all that you have learned so far, do you agree that you are the creator of your reality? And that the creation that you have made comes from your perception of the world. It comes from what you think is important.

The importance that influences your perception was created by the paradigms or beliefs of the people that influenced you and taught you about your world. It was their story that you were brought up to believe and live. You are living part of their story that has been flavoured by your experiences. If or when you become a parent, then you get to teach your children about your story! So our lives are just a story that we have about who we are and why we are the way that we are. We are all authors of a story, and right now you are living the story of your life. It is neither good or bad, right or wrong. It just is.

95% of people in this world live unconscious and therefore a reactive life. Only a few have woken up to the fact that they are the authors, the creators of their lives. Only they can determine where they are going and how they are going to feel on that journey.

When you begin to wake up to this fact, you can step back and take charge of your destiny and with all your

How Does This All Fit Together in Real Life?

tools that you now have, begin to change the road you are on and with that, change your story. Let your book of life take a new direction and bring new exciting and fulfilling experiences to your story! So when you teach your story it will have more flow and fewer struggles. It will have more self-control and power and less pain and suffering.

> *Your story is important for it shapes the future. Your story counts because people will read it!*

What we all want and need is a simple and direct way to a realization of who we are and what our purpose is. We want to understand the meaning of life so that we can realize it and feel fulfilled.

Change is the appliance that we as humans use to create progress. Change is progress, and so if individuals or organizations do not move towards change they are fated for failure. Without change we have no civilization or advancement. Our evolution has taken us from a basic existence that was almost animal like and governed by the instinct of survival to higher degrees of intelligence.

Our history has documented our continual change. We change right through our lives emotionally, mentally and physically. So change is something that is natural and normal, however when we are faced with changing our thoughts and beliefs we experience resistance. When we try to create change consciously, it feels odd, as if we are going against our normal flow of our life. Interestingly enough, we actually want to create change, so why do we resist it?

The purpose of schooling or educating our children is to teach them where we are as a society and to get them to use their mental abilities. This stimulates growth from within. Thinking promotes growth and innovation. Our brains work on the "more more" principle. The more you read, the more you want to read. The more you sit on the couch and just watch TV, the more you want to sit on the couch and watch TV.

The happier you are as a person the more you look to maintain your positive outlook. The more negative you are the more you look for evidence to support your negativity. Therefore the purpose of education is to teach an individual of their own mental potential so that they can take ownership of the outcomes of their life and have the power to solve their personal problems. The flaw in our society is that although education provides the gateway to higher intelligence for an individual, they don't teach children about their personal power and to think about their thinking. In a lot of schools children are not taught to use their own resources to overcome obstacles, and so they unconsciously learn that they are helpless and need to be helped.

Children are taught to obey and follow instructions and so very often when these children become adults they

How Does This All Fit Together in Real Life?

can't lead, they can only follow. It is what they have learned. Fortunately the world is waking up to conscious and lucid living, and systems are changing.

More and more schools are coaching children to find their own solutions, helping themselves and promoting mental growth, resilience and resolve. These children take this forward into their adulthood, the belief that they can overcome anything because they are resourceful and have a strong self-belief about what they are capable of. At the core, they feel supported and valuable, so they can accomplish anything.

When this is lacking, a change in personal belief about self-worth and ability is what is needed to create lasting change at the core, so that one can view themselves as worthy, resourceful and enough!

When you give your brain a problem, it is compelled to solve that problem. It does not matter how difficult or easy the problem is, it is going to find a way to solve it. For the same token, for every question that you give your brain; it will give you an answer.

Here is the thing: if you ask yourself stupid questions, you will get stupid answers. So because this is a response that you can always rely on, you may as well ask yourself some intelligent and resourceful questions and put your brain to good use. Give it the job it was meant to do ... to help you resolve situations, rather than to criticise how you are performing.

How Does This All Fit Together in Real Life?

Start living in the Present

What is the past? - Its gone, the past no longer exists, and the best thing about a shitty past is that it's over, it is only real in the inside world, in other words, our memories.

Where's the future? - Ahead of you, is it real? No, it's only real in your head, your inside world. Important enough to think about all the time yet, when you get to that future moment you ignore it and stress about the next possible event!

So the only thing that you have that is real right now in your life is this moment. In this moment you are sitting here reading this book. That is what is real. You could say, what is real, is that I have my family sitting at home. However you don't know that for sure. You assume that if you pick up the phone you can confirm that.

> *The truth is that the only thing that is real is this moment.*

So in this moment as you are sitting, hopefully, in the inside and outside world reading my book, do you have any problems? Ahh and breathe! Now on to the next moment, do you have any problems here?

How Does This All Fit Together in Real Life?

Living in the moment is quiet and still. In the moment we have no need to judge or change, because in the moment we are always ok and resourceful. Even when things are bad, in the moment we make decisions with the resources we have and move through the moment.

No moment ever came to stay ... they all came to pass. All moments pass. Choose wisely what they mean and how you want to feel about them.

> *This is important because your choices will shape our future.*

How Does This All Fit Together in Real Life?

How can I observe my thoughts and notice how I feel about things. Can I choose to ignore those thoughts or to feel something different? Yes, I can. I can do anything I choose to do. I can feel anything I choose to feel. I don't have to hold on to the meaning I have had till now. I am free of my past; I can live my life as I please and by doing that I will please others too. Because now I am happy and at peace. That is definitely a nice me to be with. I enjoy my own company more and feel excited to do all the things I am about to learn, for I don't fear myself anymore. I do not scare myself. I am ok, no matter what I do... and sometimes I am really wonderful!

Thank you from the bottom of my heart for reading my book. I hope it has brought you clarity to live easier and with greater purpose.

Here are some basic rules for you to live a fulfilled life:

1. Be curious to learn new things, but stop being precious about things that don't serve you.
2. Let go of parts of your story that stop you from living your dream. Live your dream and die happy and fulfilled.
3. The guarantee in life is that we are going to die. Your time on earth is short, live yours and live it with purpose. Make each day count! Invest in good thoughts.
4. Choose your thoughts, the meaning you give your thoughts and the emotions you have about them. Stop being random.
5. Know that no matter what happens and what you do, you are ok. The opinion of others is just that! Stop giving it importance above yourself.
6. Develop courage and bravery so that you can go and find a way to succeed in your life in the things that matter for you.
7. Be determined, for you are important and the world needs you.
8. Your unconscious already knows who you are and what you can do. Start to trust your decisions, your gut feelings, and your heart.

9. Change your state to solve your problems. You can't be resourceful and creative with bad brain juice.

10. Remember to become successful you need to first think yourself as if you are. Think yourself successful and your body will follow.

11. Know that your story is just a story and if it does not serve you, let it go and live your life despite of it. Life is not a dress rehearsal, so go for it; you can figure things out along the way.

12. Create an epic adventure of your life; live, laugh and have loads of fun. Be a superhero to the world, because heroes are brave and courageous and live with a purpose that is above themselves.

13. You are a bright and shining star. Stop living in the shadow of your fears. They are not real... they are just thoughts and if you observe them you will notice they just pass by.

This book is meant as a guide. In all my years of working with myself and working and teaching people the one thing that constantly came across to me, was this underlying feeling that our values and beliefs about ourselves and our lives determine how we feel about ourselves. If we can realize that they are just values and beliefs that have been passed on by others and not a universal truth about ourselves, then we have a chance to change how we feel about ourselves and what we are capable of doing.

I wish you well on your path. I hope this is going to help you live with the purpose you intended your life to have.

'And the only way to do great work is to love what you do. If you haven't found it yet, keep looking. Don't settle'.

Steve Jobs (2005)

About the Author.

Vicky Ross is the founding mind behind Vicky Ross Training and Vi'Arti!

Vicky Ross has spent her life developing herself so that she is able to teach others in the simplest of ways. Vicky understands the benefits of ongoing personal growth. She was fortunate enough to have a childhood that involved a lot of travel, which combined with her curious mind and life circumstances brought her to the belief that there had to be more to life than the 'daily struggle', there had to be a bigger purpose!

Vicky says "you are either in flow or in struggle. If you are struggling you need to ask yourself if you are in the wrong place doing the wrong thing, or the right place doing things wrong?" A constant theme that runs through all of her training is that there is no greater power to give someone than the power to be in control of themselves, and the freedom that comes from removing their limiting beliefs.

"Whatever it is; when you are working and focusing on succeeding, you start to flow and move towards success." Her quest in life is that people can live easier and lighter as a result of working with her. All her life she has had a passion for teaching, healing and helping people understand themselves better so that they can live easier.

Her main advice is to keep a curious mind, and ask yourself 'what would help make my life easier, lighter and free from limitations', and then go out there and do it!

iUnderstand Me

Human optimisation is her thing. She uses skill, knowledge, experience and her intuition to know what is happening in the core of her clients and guides them to a better life. Vicky is a Personal Growth Coach and normally works on a 1-2-1 style with her clients offering them a bespoke package to achieve optimum results.

She also specializes in organizational training, developing managers, leaders and teams to optimise their performance. Her training is always full of passion and energy, her enthusiasm for helping people understand themselves is obvious and she really enjoys helping people have those moments of realisation!

Her course specialities:

Business NLP Practitioner and Master Practitioner, Personal Development Get-aways, Advanced Language Patterns, Presentation Skills, The Art of Influence, Ericksonian Hypnotherapy, Advanced Hypnotherapy, Coaching skills for Managers, Coaching Skills for NLPer's, Good Customer Service and Facilitation Skills.

Vicky also works with children in private and in schools.

She is an assistant to Dr Richard Bandler and has worked and assisted John La Valle, Paul McKenna and Michael Neil. She is one of the few in the UK delivering a Business Practitioner license with the Society of NLP. She teaches therapists and coaches how to become even better at what they do with her expert knowledge in the language patterns to use for the elicitation of information.

iUnderstand Me

She is also a guest lecturer practitioner for Bournemouth University and has co-developed and delivers a module of Introduction to Leadership and Management for social services. Vicky is an Instructor of Hypnotherapy and teaches persuasion and influence in business.

For on going learning, Vicky has developed audio products to help individuals deal with stress, anxiety, confidence, motivation and well being.

These CD are available on her website: www.meditation-downloads.co.uk

Remember everyone can have what they want; they just need the right support and knowledge.

For more information on how Vicky can work with you individually or come and help your organization contact:

0845 026 1106
Or
email: info@vickyross.com
or visit the website:
www.vickyross-training.co.uk
www.vickyross.co.uk
www.iunderstandme.co.uk